Landscape Trees & Shrubs

LANDSCAPE TREES AND SHRUBS

Series Concept: Robert J. Dolezal
Encyclopedia Concept: Barbara K. Dolezal
Managing Editor: Victoria Cebalo Irwin
Encyclopedia Writer: Robert J. Dolezal
Photography Editor: John M. Rickard
Designer: Jerry Simon
Layout Artist: Barbara K. Dolezal
Photoshop Artist: Gerald A. Bates
Horticulturist: Peggy Henry
Photo Stylist: Peggy Henry
Proofreader: Ken DellaPenta
Index: Alta Indexing Service, El Cerrito, CA

President/CEO: Michael Eleftheriou
Vice President/Editorial: Linda Ball
Vice President/Retail Sales & Marketing: Kevin Haas

Home Improvement/*Gardening*
Executive Editor: Bryan Trandem
Editorial Director: Jerri Farris
Creative Director: Tim Himsel

Created by: Dolezal & Associates,
in partnership with Creative Publishing international, Inc.,
in cooperation with Black & Decker.
BLACK&DECKER. is a trademark of the Black & Decker
Corporation and is used under license.

Library of Congress
Cataloging-in-Publication Data

(Information on file)

ISBN 1–58923–002–7 (softcover)

PHOTOGRAPHY & ILLUSTRATION

PRINCIPAL PHOTOGRAPHY

JOHN M. RICKARD: All photographs except where otherwise noted

OTHER PHOTOGRAPHY AND ILLUSTRATION

CORBIS: ©Michael Boys, 97 (top); ©Gary W. Carter, 123 (mid); ©Eric and David Hosking, 113 (mid); ©Patrick Johns, 105 (bot), ©Richard Hamilton Smith, 107 (top)

DOUG DEALEY: pgs. 42 (bot), 66 (bot)

ROBERT J. DOLEZAL: pgs. 24 (bot), 50 (top R)

GARDENPHOTOS.COM: ©Judy White, 131 (bot)

DAVID GOLDBERG: pgs. 111 (bot), 117 (bot), 119 (bot)

DONNA KRISCHAN: pgs. vi, 2 (top R), 3, 4, 6 (top L), 13 (bot), 26 (bot), 28 (top), 29 (mid), 66 (top), 82, 86 (bot), 101 (mid), 105 (top)

FRANK LANE PICTURE AGENCY: ©Michael Rose, 115 (bot); ©Martin B. Withers, 121, (bot), 123 (bot)

NOAA: National Estuarine Research Reserve/Joan Muller, 91 (bot)

JERRY PAVIA: pgs. 7 (top R), 8 (top R), 26 (lower mid), 36 (top R), 90, 91 (mid), 92, 94, 95, 96, 97 (bot), 98, 99 (top), 100 (top), 101 (top & bot), 103 (bot), 104 (mid), 105 (mid), 106 (top), 107 (bot), 108 (top), 109 (top & bot), 110 (top & bot), 111 (top), 112 (top & mid), 113 (bot), 114 (mid), 116, 117 (top & mid), 118 (top & mid), 120 (mid & bot), 121 (top), 122 (top), 124 (bot), 125 (top), 126 (top & mid), 127 (mid & bot), 128 (top & bot), 129 (top & bot), 130 (bot), 131 (mid)

CHARLES SLAY: pg. 29 (bot)

ILLUSTRATIONS: HILDEBRAND DESIGN

ACKNOWLEDGEMENTS

The editors acknowledge with grateful appreciation the contribution to this book of Robert Menzies and Dean Pinson of Menzies' Natives Nursery, Weed, CA; and Betsy Niles, Sonoma, CA.

Landscape Trees

& Shrubs

Author
Susan Mason

Photographer
John M. Rickard

Series Concept
Robert J. Dolezal

Choosing & planting
garden trees & shrubs

CREATIVE
PUBLISHING
international

MINNETONKA, MINNESOTA

www.creativepub.com

CONTENTS

PREPARING AND PLANTING

Page 41

CARE AND MAINTENANCE

Page 63

ENCYCLOPEDIA OF TREES & SHRUBS

Page 89

RESOURCES AND INDEX

Page 132

INTRODUCTION

Trees and shrubs are at the heart of every landscape. Whether you are gardening on a rooftop or on several acres of land, trees and shrubs will form the foundation of your garden.

From dwarf Japanese maples to majestic oaks, trees are exciting and diverse, offering visual weight and sensory delight. Their leaves rustle in the breezes of spring, offer cooling shade on summer afternoons, and give us the celebratory yellow, orange, and red festival of autumn colors. Even in the winter months, when many trees are bare, they are an attractive element in your landscape, as their bark emerges as a source of beauty and their leafless branches form stark silhouettes against the sky.

Shrubs—though more diminutive than most trees—are equally varied and lovely. They can enclose a garden with a hedge of deepest

green, provide a bright and colorful accent in a yard, or scent the air with sweet fragrance.

When I first married, I moved into a home with a small, empty yard. I scarcely knew the difference between an elm and an oak, much less between a viburnum and a vitex, but I began to plant and to garden. Fifteen years later, my little corner of the earth has been transformed, and passersby often stop by the garden to admire a plant, to ask a question.

Even if you're a novice gardener, you'll soon discover your own personal style as it relates to your landscape. Indeed, you will begin to find inspiration almost everywhere you look—whether it's on a visit to an exotic locale or a trip across town. As you get ideas for your garden, jot them down in the margins of this book or in a notebook. Take snapshots of landscapes that appeal to you, or cut out pictures from magazines and collect them in a folder. When you see someone working in a garden you admire, stop and ask about the trees, shrubs and flowers.

As you read this book, I hope you feel as though I am a neighbor, leaning over the fence, chatting about the excitement and the joy of gardening with trees and shrubs—plants that will give you pleasure not just for a season, but for many years to come.

In the pages that follow, you'll find inspiration to create the garden of your dreams—whether it be a colorful patio garden brimming with fragrant shrubs or a large, wooded backyard. As you look at various types of gardens—shade gardens and sunny gardens, private retreats and public spaces—you'll discover that the most intriguing gardens are those that appeal to all of your senses. The sound of the breeze blowing in the leaves of a linden tree, the scent of a gardenia, and the pink tinge of an apple blossom all combine to make your garden not merely a thing of beauty but an experience to be savored.

You'll also discover that each tree and shrub has varied features that make it unique, from garlands of flowers to colorful seasonal foliage and fruit, from lacy textures to intriguing bark.

This chapter will show you the possibilities of container gardening and gardening in small spaces. You'll discover flowering trees and shrubs and how to plant so you'll have spectacular color in every season of the year. You'll also see how you can use plants as architectural elements, planting them in hedges, growing them as espaliers—shrubs or trees trained to grow in patterns against a blank backdrop—or pruning them in geometric forms or figures. Or you may want to simply accent a special tree in your landscape or create a living—even flowering—corridor of trees. As you survey the ideas presented here, think about what would work best in your garden. Before long, you will have developed a strong sense of what you want for your landscape and the ways in which you can accomplish your goals.

Above all, remember that gardening with trees and shrubs is a creative adventure—an ever-evolving one as your plants grow and mature. Whatever your style, you will be able to express it in your garden. Planting landscape trees and shrubs also is an act of faith, hope, and promise that you share with those around you. As you plant, you will be creating a lifetime of beauty, for yourself and for the generations that follow.

> The foundations of a garden, trees and shrubs give form—and sometimes flowers and fragrance— to every landscape

The World of Trees and Shrubs

Trees in the landscape, the most permanent of our plantings, may take generations to grow tall and mature. This sapling live oak, just placed into its hole in the bed, likely will have outlived the child that assisted in its planting by the time it reaches the size of the mature, neighboring tree behind it.

CONTAINER TREES AND SHRUBS

It is perfectly possible to create a lush garden using plants in containers. In fact, container gardening is ideal for small-space gardens such as decks, rooftops, or balconies. By layering textured plants in an assortment of sizes and shapes, you can transform any area, no matter how small, into a pleasant outdoor living space. Dwarf deciduous fruit trees or evergreen hollies planted in containers can be moved to screen a view or provide privacy, while flowering hibiscus or hardy fuchsia can provide color.

Even in expansive gardens, containers are useful: they can provide focal points, direct foot traffic, or protect a precious specimen shrub from the digging paws of a pet. In a winter garden, an evergreen conifer in a beautiful urn can become a point of interest throughout the season.

The entry area of a home almost always can be enhanced by container plantings, which add richness and intimacy. For a more dramatic effect, consider placing a small tree near your front door.

Use container plantings of shrubs to beautify small spaces in your landscape. Choose from flowering plants (above), topiaries (right), or evergreens (below).

Some of the newer dwarf magnolias often are good choices, and they provide fragrant blooms during the early summer. Camellias and gardenias also perform well in containers, lending a stately look.

When you're thinking about your container garden, keep in mind that planters themselves can create a mood. Placed in an old washtub, a rambling hydrangea is reminiscent of an old homestead, while the very same hydrangea in a Chippendale-style planter becomes quite formal. Part of the fun of container gardening, in fact, is using different planters that suit your personality. Garden centers and direct retailers carry a great assortment of containers in many styles. And found objects often make excellent planters. A wicker basket can be lined with plastic and planted with a flowering shrub, or an ornamental antique pot can house a feathery fern.

With containers, it is easy to rearrange your garden. In fact, container gardening is an excellent way to experiment with different combinations of color, leaf texture, and form. Container gardening also allows gardeners in cold climates to grow tropical plants outdoors during the summer, since they can be brought indoors to overwinter.

URBAN AND SMALL-SPACE GARDENS

Gardens that are precious for their size benefit by addition of the vertical accents of trees and shrubs. Use them for color—either flowers or distinctive foliage (left)—add a sculpted bonsai to a table in an apartment (below), or create an overhead canopy of trees to shelter an urban courtyard and provide shade (bottom).

Urban and small-space gardens can be made as soothing and serene as their country counterparts. Courtyard gardens, patio plantings, and rooftop gardens invite attention to detail, and with that comes an appreciation of even the smallest attribute of a plant. Since a plant such as a Japanese maple will be viewed up close in a small garden, you are more likely to notice the unfurling of a leaf in spring, the finely dissected nature of each feathery leaf in summer, and the intricate branching structure of the stems in winter. Likewise, the fragrance of even the most delicately scented flower will be pronounced in a small garden. The small, lightly scented white flowers of a holly, for example, rarely noticed in large landscapes until its red berries appear at the end of autumn, will be right there for you to enjoy in a small space.

When selecting plants for a small garden, keep scale and perspective in mind. A few choice selections of midsized trees or shrubs will help an urban garden feel expansive, but the heart of a small garden rests in the many dwarf and miniature species of trees and shrubs that are now available. *Itea* 'Little Henry' is a dwarf version of the old-fashioned sprawler Virginia sweetspire, with racemes of pure white flowers in early summer and brilliant red foliage in autumn. Similarly, the diminutive *Spiraea* 'Gold Mound' with its bright yellow foliage will fit well into nearly any garden.

Small gardens are especially well suited to themed plantings. For instance, English gardener Vita Sackville-West's famous White Garden at Sissinghurst has been an inspiration to many, and her scheme of silver-foliaged plants juxtaposed with white-blooming shrubs and flowers brings elegance to any setting. A different theme, but one that is equally appealing, might be to re-create a tropical paradise on your patio, replete with bird-of-paradise, bougainvillea, and potted date palms. Whatever theme you choose, it will tie the disparate elements of your garden together to create a cohesive whole.

FLOWERING TREES AND SHRUBS

Flowering trees and shrubs appeal to our senses by adding both color and fragrance to a garden. Certainly each of us has a special memory of a flowering plant—perhaps you remember delicate cherry blossoms declaring the arrival of spring, or smile at the memory of a summer evening sweetened by the intense fragrance of gardenia. Indeed, many researchers think that color and fragrance are our two most primal and instinctive senses, that some people gravitate toward soft pastels, while others seem inextricably drawn to bright and vivid hues. And the scent of a freshly mown lawn can transport many an adult back to childhood almost instantly.

When planning for color in the landscape, remember that the blooms on most flowering shrubs and trees are seasonal, lasting at most for several weeks or perhaps a month. But by selecting plants that bloom in sequence, you can create a garden that shines with color throughout much of the year. The range of bloom colors is wide, stretching from the pure white of a flowering pear to the deep and vivid purple of a Formosa azalea. Be sure to select a color palette that not only appeals to you but that looks good against the backdrop of your home. The white blooms of an oakleaf hydrangea nicely echo the white trim on a house, while the carmine blooms of certain spiraeas complement a home with red shutters.

Trees and shrubs that bear colorful flowers both beautiful and fragrant are a true windfall.

(Above and inset) Rhododendron and azalea are showy when in bloom; for the remainder of the season, they are foundation shrubs bearing lovely green foliage and with dense texture.

(Right) Flowering crabapple is a good choice for early bloom in cold-winter climates where it flowers soon after leaves appear. Here, the cultivar is 'Snowdrift'.

(Right inset) Crabapple cultivars are available in red, as pictured here, as well as in pink, purple, and white.

From spicy to sweet, from citrusy to musky, fragrance can transform any garden into an enchanting place. To make your garden a treat for the senses, consider adding at least one fragrant plant for each season. For example, in spring, lilacs and Korean spice viburnum exude delightful, lingering scents. The highly perfumed flowers of gardenia, magnolia, and sweet shrub are good choices to make summer nights memorable, while oleaster radiates an intoxicating fragrance in autumn. In winter or very early spring, when color and scent are particularly welcome, daphne and witch-hazel open small but aromatic blooms.

SEASONAL COLOR

One of the glories of a garden is that it is ever changing. Every season brings something new in terms of color, and each season has its own distinctive palette. Spring is the season of fresh color. The soft light of the season makes colors seem clear and pure, making them easy to work with in the landscape.

One way to use color in the garden is to take cues from nature. In a woodland or prairie in spring, pinks, whites, yellows, and other soft colors predominate. Introducing these colors to your garden will bring the delights of the season to your doorstep. Dogwoods with creamy white blooms, silver-bells with pendant clusters of snow white flowers, and flowering pears and crabapples with their soft pinkish flowers are all trees that flower in spring. Many shrubs also put on a lovely spring show. The arching yellow branches of forsythia herald the season, appearing at the same time as many daffodils. Azaleas, mock orange, flowering quince, and weigela come into bloom soon after.

In summer, the warm sun brings bright colors to the fore, at the same time making the cooling greens of foliage particularly appealing. The yellow flower clusters of the golden-chain tree appear in early summer, while the watermelon red or salmon pink blooms of crape myrtles come slightly later. Butterfly bush, cinquefoil, hypericum, and lilac bloom colorfully, either alone or in mixed beds with brightly hued perennials and annuals.

In autumn, the slanting sun makes the sunset colors of the season all the more pleasing. Fiery reds, glowing oranges, and intense yellows blaze forth from dogwoods, ginkgos, maples, oaks, and sweet-gums. To create a picturesque autumn display, you can repeat the brilliant hues of these trees with underplantings of shrubs whose foliage also changes color in autumn. Among the plants that you might consider are arrowwood, burning bush, enkianthus, fothergilla, and sweetspire, all of which offer a kaleidoscope of autumn foliage that complements their larger kin.

Even in winter, the garden can be a source of beautiful hues. Winter color comes largely from the green of evergreens, the berries of fruiting plants, and bark. Although most trees and shrubs have bark in the gray to brown range—which can be beautiful in itself—some bear bark of striking red or yellow. Red-twig dogwood and golden willow are two widely planted examples, and both work as exclamation points in the subdued winter garden.

(Left and inset) Maples and sweet-gums are fiery in autumn when their leaves begin to turn.

(Below and inset) Ginkgo—also called maidenhair tree—has the spectacular habit of first turning brilliant yellow in a display that lasts for weeks, then suddenly losing all of its leaves at once in a 1- or 2-day span.

HAVENS AND RETREATS

(Right) Recent plantings of cypress will soon screen this patio from the house that neighbors it.

(Below and inset) Choices range from a natural garden of trees, background shrubs, and annual flowers to a formal planting with sheared hedges.

Through the imaginative use of trees and shrubs, you can create a personal and inviting garden retreat. The uses of a retreat will vary from person to person and from season to season, but the basic concepts underlying the creation of any haven remain the same.

Think first of what type of retreat you want and how you plan to use it. You may want a *giardino segreto*—Italian for "secret garden"—for children to play in and discover the delights of nature. Or you might want a sheltered glade where you can spread a blanket and enjoy a picnic lunch. Perhaps you dream of a quiet sitting area where you can sit and read a book all alone, or of a garden that re-creates a special place that you remember from childhood. For some people an ideal retreat will be lush but loosely structured, while for others refuge will be an Oriental meditation garden, which evinces simplicity by the restrained and subtle use of the plants selected.

Regardless of style, certain aspects of a garden retreat remain constant. Almost by definition, retreats are enclosed for privacy. Hedges or fences planted with climbing vines are ideal for this purpose. Depending on your site, you may want the hedge or fence to be dense and impenetrable to ensure complete privacy, or you may prefer a more open planting that gives the sense of enclosure without blocking pleasant breezes. Overhead canopies of arching tree limbs lend intimacy to a retreat while providing shade and shelter underneath.

You'll most likely want to add chairs, benches, or a swing to your hideaway. Painted, weathered chairs lend country charm, for example, while carved teak benches make a more formal statement. You may also want to add a water feature. A fountain that gurgles with the cool splash of falling water gently animates a garden retreat, while a quiet reflection pond pulls the sky into the garden and adds a sense of tranquillity.

Close your eyes and think of your ideal yard. If you're like most people, you'll have pictured a landscape that includes tall, leafy trees providing cooling shade to you and your home. After all, shade trees are icons throughout the world. Who can imagine a summer afternoon picnic without people seeking shelter from the sun under the shade of a tree, or an old country home without a giant oak or beech standing sentry in the yard, providing cooling protection to the home's front porch and shade for its windows?

You may already have trees in your yard, or you may be starting from scratch. Even if you are beginning with a blank slate, you can have shade sooner than you might have imagined possible: planting trees carries blessings to future generations, but fortunately, the benefits accrue quickly. Most shade trees will give a reasonable degree of protection from the sun within 5 to 7 years of planting, and some fast-growing trees may provide shade even more swiftly.

If you already have shady areas in your garden, you can create a lush oasis in filtered light. Ferns, hostas, and annuals such as impatiens make a shady spot even more inviting on a warm summer day, and there are many shrubs, including mahonia and rhododrendron, that flourish in shade as well. A bed of azaleas next to a child's sandbox can add a wave of summer color to the play area, or the leaves of a variegated hydrangea can bring a luminous quality to the shade even after the sun goes down.

For more enjoyment, add a few finishing touches. If you have children, think about installing a swing for them. On the other hand, if your shady oasis is for your own enjoyment, you may want to add a hammock. You can hang it between two sturdy tree trunks or mount it on a stand. Either way, plant a patch of shade-loving mint nearby, and you can enjoy minted iced tea or juleps while you lounge. What more could you ask for on a warm summer afternoon?

SHADE GARDENS

(Left) The shade from a tree can be put to many uses, from children's play to an informal picnic.

(Below and inset) Careful placement of junipers in a woodland yard give support to this hammock. In a quiet spot, boxwood shades a bench and hydrangea surrounds it with blooms.

SPECIMENS AND ALLÉES

(Right) An allée of stately trees lines a path beneath their canopy.

(Below and inset) Specimen trees are striking both during the day and at night. It's best to choose a featured location for planting large landscape trees.

Two time-honored ways to add visual interest to your landscape are through the use of specimen plants and allées. Specimen plants are trees or shrubs that are planted alone in the landscape as accents. In contrast, an allée consists of two parallel rows of trees or shrubs planted to create a corridor.

A specimen plant can be a large majestic tree, a delicate ornamental tree, or a particularly noteworthy shrub placed in the landscape as a free-standing, eye-catching focal point. A good specimen plant will provide dramatic interest throughout the year by virtue of its outstanding form, size, foliage, flowers, or fruit. In an expansive lawn, a copper beech, with its reddish bronze foliage and height of nearly 75 feet (23 m), can serve as an accent and provide

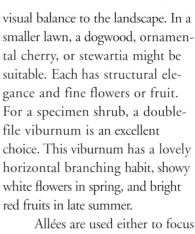

visual balance to the landscape. In a smaller lawn, a dogwood, ornamental cherry, or stewartia might be suitable. Each has structural elegance and fine flowers or fruit. For a specimen shrub, a double-file viburnum is an excellent choice. This viburnum has a lovely horizontal branching habit, showy white flowers in spring, and bright red fruits in late summer.

Allées are used either to focus attention on a distant object or to create an elegant corridor through which to walk from one part of the garden to another. Traditionally associated with English estates, allées can work magically even in compact areas. Imagine walking through a tunnel of blooming Yoshino cherry trees, with a canopy of snowy white blossoms enveloping you and a series of graceful trunks leading you on. Such a beautiful and well-designed allée makes even the smallest space seem expansive.

Hedges act much like fences in a landscape, but they add a dynamic feel that fences do not. Hedges can be used to create privacy, separate one part of the garden from another, screen unwanted views, define a garden space, or create a backdrop for colorful flowers. Depending on the plants used, hedges can be formal or rustic, soft to the touch or prickly, imposing or diminutive. Single rows of sheared plants give an architectural look, while loose plantings of shrubs that have been shaped only lightly are more natural looking.

Topiary is the practice of pruning plants into geometric shapes or into more intricate forms such as elephants, rabbits, or teapots. It is an ancient art that was very popular in medieval times and is still quite common, particularly in European landscapes. You can incorporate topiary by placing spiraled junipers on either side of your entryway or by using an obelisk-shaped yew as a special focal point.

Espalier is the art of training a tree or shrub to grow flat against a wall, trellis, or fence. Excellent for small courtyard gardens as well as large gardens, such plants add beauty and interest to a blank wall. An espalier is created by training a young tree or shrub to grow into a desired design—be it a diamond pattern, a fan shape, or the form of a candelabra—when the branches are still soft and pliable. The shape is maintained over the years by careful pruning.

HEDGES, TOPIARY, AND ESPALIER

(Left) Neat pruning of a formal hedge and shrub border is a frame to the loose appearance of perennial flowers.

(Bottom) A yard planted with shrubs surrounded by a gravel mulch is easy to maintain.

(Inset) A whimsical evergreen topiary spirals in a container.

I

nspired by ideas in the previous chapter, you're now ready to begin translating your dreams into reality. Perhaps the best way to do that is to look at your landscape as would a professional designer. In the following pages, you'll find a garden planner's approach to assessing your site and its potential.

The first step is to examine your site's physical and environmental characteristics. While many aspects of gardening are universal, others are profoundly influenced by regional and local conditions. The trees and shrubs that thrive in a cold mountainous environment are very different from those that flourish in a tropical climate. By knowing what grows in your corner of the world and planting what does best, you'll create a garden that is both beautiful and healthy.

In this chapter, you'll also be asked to consider some basic questions about what you want to achieve in a garden. Do you want to create cooling shade on hot, sunny days? Do you want to enclose your garden with a stately evergreen hedge? Is it important to have a grassy sward for children to play on, or would you prefer a no-mow yard where ground covers and shrubs take center stage? Your answers to these fundamental questions are the criteria you will use in designing the garden that suits you and your family.

Once these basics are covered, you'll delve into some fundamental principles of landscape design, such as unity and scale. You will learn the rudiments of selecting healthy trees and shrubs that are adapted to your site and look at some of the tools you'll need as you head out to your yard, garden gloves in hand. Since gardening is an ongoing learning experience, you will also discover several excellent sources of additional gardening information and inspiration.

In the final pages of this chapter, you'll find a Tree and Shrub Planning Flowchart—a handy guide you'll want to refer to as you embark on your garden project. It summarizes the main points you'll need to consider to ensure that your landscape becomes the attractive, healthy environment you envision.

Plan, prepare, and establish your goals— important steps to a successful garden

Checklist for Trees and Shrubs

A successful tree and shrub border begins by carefully evaluating your landscape site, selecting the right plants, and obtaining advice to help you in your planning.

SITE AND SOIL

The secret to successful gardening is to place the right plant in the right spot. The key is to evaluate your site and its soil, and then select trees and shrubs that are well suited to your particular landscape.

When gardeners talk about site, they're referring to all the various factors that affect growing conditions—the type of soil, the average humidity, the amount of rainfall, the number of days of sun per year, the elevation, and the garden's climate zone [see USDA Plant Hardiness Zones Around the World, pg. 132]. Within your overall site, each plant occupies its own place—be it sunny or shady, subject to strong winds or protected from gusty blasts, dry or wet [see Analyzing Your Site, pg. 32].

(Right) A hillside can be planted with trees by terracing it with individual level planting holes.

(Inset) Choose deep-rooted trees for street and roadway plantings.

(Bottom) Take all of your site's conditions into consideration, including direction of prevailing winds, sun exposure, and its soil.

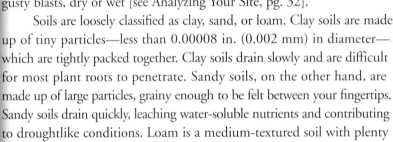

Soils are loosely classified as clay, sand, or loam. Clay soils are made up of tiny particles—less than 0.00008 in. (0.002 mm) in diameter—which are tightly packed together. Clay soils drain slowly and are difficult for most plant roots to penetrate. Sandy soils, on the other hand, are made up of large particles, grainy enough to be felt between your fingertips. Sandy soils drain quickly, leaching water-soluble nutrients and contributing to droughtlike conditions. Loam is a medium-textured soil with plenty of humus—decomposed organic matter. Loam is easy to work and is a good growing medium for nearly all plants. Soils have varying degrees of acidity or alkalinity—or pH—which easily is determined by a soil test [see Testing Soil, pg. 33].

Most plants are best suited to a single site condition and soil type. Plants generally thrive in areas where the climate and soil are similar to their native habitat: a shrub such as oleander, which is native to the Mediterranean, does best in warm areas, while a tree such as balsam fir, which grows naturally in wet soils in the northern United States and Canada, does best in colder, damper regions. Arborvitae and junipers are adapted to sandy soils, while alder, kerria, and sassafras grow well in clay. Fortunately, for every site there is a wide array of well-adapted plants.

Before you take spade in hand, assess your desires and goals, taking an inventory of the existing landscape features. In CHAPTER 3: Designing Tree and Shrub Landscapes, you'll learn how to draw a garden plan, but now it's time to daydream. Walk into your yard or your patio. What do you see that you like? What's missing? Do you want a tree to provide seasonal shade? Would you like a secluded area with a small garden bench or a sunny play area for children? Do you want to soften the architecture of your home, hide a utility meter, or add a fragrant shrub near the entrance to welcome guests? Is seasonal color what you're after? Or perhaps you will select trees for the flowers they bear in spring or the fruit that ripens on their limbs in summer.

Think about the functional areas since they will affect your choice of planting material. For example, a vegetable garden needs plenty of sun to flourish. If you have a vegetable patch, you'll need to place new trees so that even when the trees are mature there will still be plenty of sun to ripen tomatoes. If you have a swimming pool or plan to install one, you'll want to avoid trees that drop leaves and other debris, opting instead for shrubs and small trees to ring the area.

Consider also your favorite time of day for being in the garden. If morning coffee on the patio appeals to you, you'll want early-morning sun to light your patio. In this case, small trees and shrubs should be planted East of your patio, while a shade tree could go to the West. For enjoyment at twilight you'll want to select plants whose strong points shine at dusk; white flowers and variegated plants both come to the fore in fading light.

If your home is on a busy street, a hedge can add privacy and make your garden more peaceful. A site exposed to strong winds may benefit from a windbreak—some pines are a good choice—while a home with a fabulous view will be enhanced by plantings that frame the vista and complement it to its best advantage.

YOUR PURPOSE, NEEDS, AND REQUIREMENTS

(Left) Consider how your garden will appear in each season. These flowering plum trees celebrate spring's warmth.

(Inset) Firethorn berries appear in summer, a food favorite for many songbirds.

(Bottom) Picture your landscape in autumn, but keep in mind the sculptural nature of its bare branches for winter.

PLANNING FOR CARE

As you plan your landscape, imagine yourself in the years to come, being outdoors and enjoying the beautiful yard you've designed and nourished. Now is the time to zero in on that aspect of gardening and ask yourself some questions.

Does a weekend of puttering around your garden, pruning hedges and edging beds, sound relaxing and peaceful, or does your ideal weekend revolve around sitting quietly on a garden bench and reading a good book? Do you look forward to donning garden gloves and pulling out a shovel, or would you choose to enlist the help of a professional? Once you've decided how many hours a week or a month you'd like to spend maintaining your landscape, let that guide you in defining the scope of your project and creating your planting scheme.

Low-maintenance plantings are typically more naturalistic than formal. They feature natural areas of shrubsvand trees and expanses of easy-care ground covers. These landscapes contain native plants or plants that are well adapted to the climate; this reduces required labor because well-adapted plants need little coddling and stay healthier than do non-adapted plants. Plants are also selected with their mature height in mind. This way future pruning will be minimized. For example, a low-maintenance garden might contain a mass of dwarf heavenly bamboo below a living room window, so that even at the plants' maturity the view from inside will be unobstructed.

If you relish every bit of daylight for the time it gives you to garden, you might follow many low-maintenance landscape principles but give yourself some challenges. You might create a topiary, grow a shrub that needs extra winter protection, or maintain a formal hedge. Whatever type of garden you choose, it's important to match your capabilities and availability with the maintenance needs of your future landscape.

(Below) Plant care tags usually are found attached to your trees and shrubs by the growers. These tags cite useful selection and care data for the plants.

(Bottom) As you plan, remember to consider the regular care that formal plantings will require. Here, a boxwood hedge will need pruning at least twice during each garden season.

Although you'll look at garden design in more detail later in this book, it's helpful to start thinking about some basic design fundamentals even in the early planning stages. Among the most important principles are unity, scale, and shape.

LANDSCAPE DESIGN: UNITY, SCALE, AND SHAPE

Unity, or harmony, is at the heart of design. All the elements in the landscape—features, fences, patios, plants, structures, and walkways—should work together to create your overall style. Examine the elements you already have and enhance them with complementary plants and materials. For a southwestern-style home, suitable plants might include rugged pines, yuccas, and other plants unique to the American southwest. On the other hand, lilacs and sweet viburnum might be most harmonious in the garden of a charming Victorian bungalow. Similar unifying effects can be achieved with non-plant materials. For instance, if you have a brick home, you might want to echo the brick in a walkway, patio, or bed edging to tie the landscape together visually.

(Left) The charm of this tree and shrub bed stems from each of the plants it contains and their individual appearance. Their forms, sizes, and growth habits balance to achieve the desired, pleasing result.

(Below) The unique coloration of a Japanese maple makes it stand out as a central feature, a focal point for the bench.

Another important design element is scale—the size relationship between objects. The size of your plantings should be compatible with the scale of your house. A tree such as a dogwood, which is of medium height and has an open habit, is a good choice for the corner of a small house. Taller trees and denser shrubs balance and anchor larger homes set in more expansive surroundings.

Finally, as you plan your landscape, it is helpful to think of plants in terms of shape. Shrubs are columnar, rounded, spiky, mounding, or fastigiated—tall and narrowing toward the top. Likewise, trees are often classified as columnar, pendulous, pyramidal, round-crowned, vase-shaped, or weeping. Let these shapes become mental templates. Use them to decide on the plants you'll use to complement your house. You may choose a tall pyramidal tree to soften a corner, a mass of mounding shrubs under the front windows, and a weeping tree as an accent. Look at your site, consider the appearance you desire, then choose the species that fits. When it comes time to acquire plants, make your shopping list, matching your mental templates with particular trees and shrubs that are adapted to your area and are of the size and shape you desire.

OPTIONS AND SELECTION

Selecting plants for your landscape is an exciting project—you are finally going to translate your ideas into reality. But as you choose different trees and shrubs, you'll want to make sure they are appropriate for your site. Be assured that for every place in your garden, there is a plant that will suit your needs exactly.

One important criterion in plant selection is whether a tree or shrub is hardy in your area—that is, whether the plant will survive for many years in your garden. To a large degree, hardiness is determined by average temperatures. For example, a camellia that is hardy in Georgia may be less so in Alberta, where the winter temperatures are much lower. Likewise, a blue spruce, which grows well across most of Canada, is less suited to Florida, where the summer temperatures are high. The primary guide to plant hardiness is the USDA Plant Hardiness Zone map [see Plant Hardiness, right].

In addition to hardiness zone ratings, you'll want to consider other factors as well. If you live in an arid region, select plants adapted to dry conditions. If you garden in a coastal area, choose plants adapted to sandy soils and saline breezes. Local nursery and garden center staff and extension service agents are all helpful, as is the plant encyclopedia at the back of this book [see Encyclopedia of Landscape Trees & Shrubs, pg. 89].

A final detail to consider is the microclimate in which you plan to place your tree or shrub. Every yard or patio, no matter how small, has microclimates—areas that are a few degrees warmer or cooler than their general surroundings, or areas that are more windy or more protected than others. You can use these microclimates to good advantage. Shrubs and trees that bear tender blooms in early spring can be protected from late frosts if placed in a sheltered spot. Conversely, you can encourage early bloom on flowering trees and shrubs by placing the plants in a warm, sunny exposure.

PLANT HARDINESS

The United States Department of Agriculture (USDA) divides North America and other areas of the world into 11 plant hardiness zones [see Plant Hardiness Around the World, pg. 132]. The zones, based on average minimum annual temperatures, serve as a general guide to growing conditions. Trees and shrubs are rated as to the zones for which they are best adapted—for example, zones 4–7—and these are usually listed on plant labels and in plant encyclopedias.

Determine the microclimates in your yard by observation. After a light snow, the spots that melt first are in warm microclimates, while snows linger in cold microclimates. Gardeners in mild-winter climates can note which parts of the garden have the first spring growth. Locations nearest a structure are typically a few degrees warmer than exposed areas, and low spots tend to be colder than high areas.

Many conifer evergreens are hardy in cold-winter climates. They remain green in the winter landscape long after deciduous trees have lost their leaves.

(Above) Three signs of healthy new trees and shrubs: vibrant green foliage (top), supple limbs (middle), and vitality (above).

(Right) Options for trees include bare-root plants (top), boxed or containerized (right), and balled-and-burlapped (inset).

CHOOSING HEALTHY TREES AND SHRUBS

When the time comes to acquire your new trees and shrubs, you can order from a direct merchant's catalog, make purchases through the electronic marketplace, or shop at a local nursery or garden center. In any case, it pays to find a quality merchant. If you shop at a local nursery or garden center, take a look around. Are the aisles clean and merchandise neatly displayed? Do the plants look healthy overall? Is the staff knowledgeable? Generally, a retailer who pays attention to these details is a good bet to stock healthy plants.

Depending on where you obtain your plants, you may have a choice between balled-and-burlapped plants, bare-root plants, or those grown in containers; all are excellent options. If you are selecting plants during the growing season and have the chance to visually inspect them, first look at the leaves. They should have good color, without any discoloration. If it is the dormant season, gently bend the twigs: healthy twigs have some spring to them and should bend rather than snap.

You should also examine the plant's root system. After asking the nursery or garden center staff for permission, place the plant on its side and carefully slide part of the rootball out of its container. Some roots, whitish in color, should be visible on the outside of the rootball. If the roots are dark brown, badly tangled, or encircling the pot, the plant should be skipped over.

When it comes to trees and shrubs, resist the temptation to choose the largest plant you can find. Research shows that the smaller the tree or shrub is when you plant it, the better it will adapt to your climate and the healthier it will be in the long run. Besides, you'll find that smaller, younger plants in 1-gallon (3.8-l) or 5-gallon (18.9-l) containers also are more economical, and they're easier to transport and carry to your planting site than are larger, more mature trees and shrubs.

TOOLS AND MATERIALS

Specialty tools are a must when you care for shrubs and trees. Consider a pole pruner that can reach into tall trees (below), or additions from this collection (bottom, clockwise from top): hedge trimmer, wheelbarrow, axe, lopping shears, leaf blower, foldable pruning saw, string trimmer, shovel, spade, and garden rake.

Having the proper tools helps make gardening a pleasure. Basics include a good shovel, a rake, a hand trowel, and a watering can. Depending on the size of the area you are gardening and the terrain, you may also want a wheelbarrow for hauling heavy items, a mattock for breaking hard-packed soils, or a hoe for weeding and leveling soil. When it comes time to prune, you'll need hand pruners, lopping shears, and a pruning saw [see Pruning Tools, pg. 65].

As you select gardening tools, choose those that fit you. Try each tool on for size in the store. Long-handled shovels work well for many people, but short-handled tools sometimes suit petites better. Likewise, hand tools should feel comfortable to hold and have a pleasant heft. Hand shears and trowels come in different sizes, and many have contoured or padded handles designed for extra comfort.

Always opt for quality tools. They will serve you well in the garden, and with proper care they will last for many years. Choose a shovel with a steel-tempered blade that's solidly fastened to a smooth, rounded handle. The top of the blade should have a rolled edge; it will be comfortable to step down on while you are digging. Look for shears and loppers with cutting edges that are solid, sharp, and well aligned, and hand pruners with a locking mechanism that is easy to operate. A wheelbarrow or garden cart should have sturdy wheels, good maneuverability, and a basin large enough to hold the items you plan to haul.

Soil amendments, fertilizers, garden hoses and any irrigation supplies, tree stakes and guy wires, and other helpful items such as gardening gloves all are available at nurseries or retail garden centers. For specialized tools such as power augers, saws, and tillers, keep in mind that often they can be rented at hardware stores or rental centers.

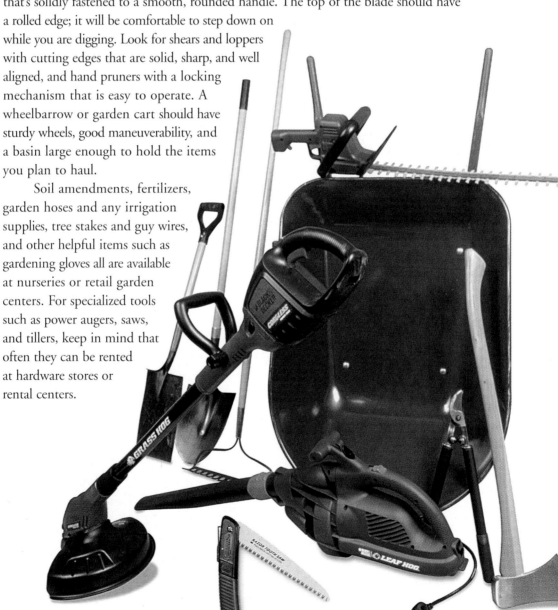

One of the great joys of gardening is that it invites a lifelong love of learning. There is always something new and exciting to discover. Whether you are just beginning to garden or have been involved in the hobby for many years, one of the best sources of expert information is your local nursery or garden retailer. Reputable garden centers are staffed with well-trained personnel who understand the specifics of your area's soil, climate, and regional conditions. Retailers stock plants that are well suited to your area, and their staff can knowledgeably answer a range of questions on topics from soil amendments to a particular plant's care needs. Another valuable resource is the USDA or Agriculture Canada Cooperative Extension service, plus those at local universities. Regional offices of these extension services produce a wide array of printed material dealing with gardening issues in your area, and extension agents, who are familiar with the latest scientific research, are available to answer gardening questions. Some offices use trained volunteer Master Gardeners to assist or advise home gardeners.

One of the most delightful ways to increase your knowledge of trees and shrubs is to visit botanical gardens and arboretums—gardens that focus on trees. Operated throughout the world, these feature collections of plants maintained for public display and scientific study. A trip to a botanical garden allows you to see a variety of plants and to develop ideas for your own. To view a display of mature trees can be a real bonus when you are planning your own landscape. And since education is an important goal of most botanical gardens, you may be able to sign up for classes, take advantage of the offerings in the library or bookstore, or ask questions of a staff horticulturist while you are visiting. Community colleges and university extensions often offer gardening and horticulture classes as well.

With a computer, horticultural information is right at your fingertips. Among the many electronic information sources, many growers, gardening clubs, and individual hobbyists have an active presence, and many growers offer tips as well as products. The appendix at the end of this book lists a number of electronic sites to get you started [see On-Line, pg. 134].

Other media outlets are also good resources. A visit to your local newsstand or bookstore will net you a variety of magazines and books ranging from plant encyclopedias and landscape design manuals to books on specific aspects of gardening. Many metropolitan newspapers feature weekly columns about gardening issues, usually written by local experts. Some cable television stations offer programs devoted to the home garden, while radio stations often feature call-in shows during the weekend. Listening to these programs is akin to taking a university course in gardening. Before you know it, you'll be answering your neighbor's questions!

(Above) Traditional reference books are a good starting point for learning about plants. They are available in bookstores and in local libraries.

(Below) Electronic resources also are helpful when choosing plants. Their information is current and frequently is provided by growers who specialize in the plants they describe.

TREES AND SHRUBS PLANNING FLOWCHART

A flowchart is a written checklist that allows you to quickly scan all the major decisions that should be reviewed as you start a garden project. The checklist presented here deals with the factors you'll need to consider as you undertake tree and shrub plantings. A little time spent reviewing your project with this chart will ensure your landscape planting is a success.

UNDERSTANDING YOUR SITE

1 **Site Consideration Questions:** What are the climate conditions where you live, and in which USDA hardiness zone are you located? What type of soil do you have? Is it rich with nutrients, or does it require amendments? Is your site exposed to strong winds, or is it sheltered? Have you identified your site's microclimate? Is it sunny or shady? Is your home on a busy street, or does it neighbor a green space? Will you need new garden features, structures, or paths? Are there any local codes, zoning restrictions, or homeowner association requirements to consider?

DETERMINING GOALS

2 **Objective and Goal Questions:** What do you want to achieve with your tree and shrub plantings? Do you wish to create shade by planting large trees, increase privacy by adding an evergreen hedge, or block the wind with a windbreak? Do you want to enhance your home with well-placed foundation plantings? Do you want to add color to your landscape by including flowering shrubs or trees with beautiful autumn color? How will your garden be used and by whom? How do you want to express your personal style in the garden?

PROJECT PLANNING AND GARDEN SYSTEMS

3 **Planning Questions:** Have you transferred your goals to paper by developing a master garden plan? As you take pen to paper, ask yourself the following questions: Does your base map accurately show all your garden's existing features? Does it include garden systems such as electricity, plumbing, and lighting? Does it incorporate each of your objectives? Does your plan utilize basic design principles such as unity, scale, and shape? Be sure to take your time with the plan, until you get it just the way you want it.

4 Implementation Questions:

Now that you have a plan, it's time to decide exactly how you will implement it. Is it the correct season for planting in your area, or would it be better to wait until a different time of year? Do you have the time and resources to implement your plan all at once, or would you rather tackle the landscape one section at a time? If you have decided on an incremental approach, which part of your plan will you complete first? How long will each phase take? What is the budget for each phase of your plan? How long will it take you to install the project? Where will you turn for advice or help? Will you implement your plan alone or seek professional assistance?

ORGANIZING TIME AND RESOURCES

SOIL PREPARATION, MATERIALS, AND TOOLS

5 Preparation Questions:

Do you have any existing landscape elements—plants or structures—to be removed? Have you assessed your soil's texture, and has the soil been tested for fertility and pH? If you are installing a shrub border, does the soil need to be improved with amendments? Do you have on hand all the tools and materials required for your project? If you plan to install any systems such as irrigation or lighting, have you obtained the necessary components? When will you build raised beds or install berms? When will you obtain your trees and shrubs? If you need assistance with any aspect of your project, have you enlisted the aid of friends or sought professional help?

CHOOSING YOUR TREES AND SHRUBS

6 Selection and Planting Questions:

Where will you obtain your trees and shrubs? Is the source reputable, and is it neat and orderly? Will each tree or shrub you are choosing have the height, shape, and form you desire at its maturity? Is it well adapted to your growing area and to the sun exposure it will receive? Do its maintenance requirements match your lifestyle? Have you examined the plant's top growth and root system to make sure it's healthy? Before actually planting the trees and shrubs, will you place them in their planned spaces in the landscape and assess their placement, making any changes as necessary?

Discover the varied features of trees and shrubs, examine your site, then begin to plan your haven

Designing Tree and Shrub Landscapes

N ow that you have a good idea of the creative possibilities, your site's potential, and your personal style and desires, you can put pencil to paper to decide exactly how to achieve your goals.

In this chapter, you'll take a closer look at the role of trees and shrubs in the landscape, and at the special uses of deciduous and evergreen plants. You'll explore exciting ways to use color to enliven your landscape, and see how to select flowering trees and shrubs that will bloom beautifully in your area. You'll be introduced to new ways of expressing your personal style through the use of plant shape and texture in your garden, and see how to create optical illusions with plants. You'll also look at the practical side of planting hedgerows to make your garden a more peaceful, sheltered area.

Once again you will turn to your site, making a final, fine-tuned analysis of factors such as sun exposure and soil moisture levels. Then you'll begin to sketch out a garden plan, bringing together everything you know about your site and your goals. Here the fun truly begins, as you experiment with all the many possibilities. Sketch out a border of flowering shrubs curving along your walkway, and see how it looks. Or draw an allée of cherry trees along your driveway, and consider if it suits you. Do you want a bench in your new garden? Add one to your plan, placing it here and there until you find just the right spot for it.

Remember that now is the time to test your design ideas. Designing a garden is an ongoing creative endeavor rather than a sequential task or one that will be completed in a single day. As you try out your ideas, thoughts will come to you, you will pick up your eraser, and you will start new sketches that reflect the changes. Your garden plan will change and mature as you muse over the possibilities, see other gardens that you admire, discover new trees and shrubs, and become more familiar with your gardening space, defining your plans and filling your needs.

Working with a landscape designer is a sure way to achieve a professional result; with a little effort, you also can do the job yourself. Gather all your reference materials, sketch pads, drawing tools, and your ideas, then begin by planning how each part of your tree and shrub landscape will be used.

TREES IN THE LANDSCAPE

Trees give a landscape a sense of permanence and maturity. But their towering presence is more than just pleasing to the eye—they affect the environment in several significant ways. Tree roots aerate and stabilize the soil, while their foliage shields the ground from the noonday sun. Trees increase the humidity of their surroundings by giving off water vapor, and through the biological process known as photosynthesis, they remove carbon dioxide from the air and replace it with life-giving oxygen.

When it comes to planning for trees in your landscape, start by evaluating your needs and desires, since what you want to accomplish will affect the type of tree you'll select. Keep in mind that shade trees are typically the dominant element in a landscape. Many shade trees grow to 80 feet (24 m) or more in height, with a spread of 50 feet (15 m) or more. Vase-shaped trees

(Right) Mature trees that stand alone frame structures and are strong vertical elements in a shrub and flower landscape.

(Below) Privacy is precious when your home is on a busy street. Use trees and shrubs to create a screen. They block your home from sight and provide a filtered view from interior windows. Choose shrubs and trees armed with thorns if security also is an issue.

such as elms and Japanese zelkova, rounded trees such as white oak and eastern white pine, and some oval trees such as lindens make good shade trees since their crowns are wide enough to cast broad shadows. In contrast, tall and columnar trees are put to their best use when only slender shadows are desired.

The tree's planned location in the landscape will also influence your selection. Some trees such as white fir and European hornbeam are clean in habit—they shed little debris onto the ground underneath—making them good choices to plant near walkways, patios, or parking areas. Other trees such as oak or tupelo shed acorns, seedpods, or staining fruits and are therefore better planted at the periphery of your property or in areas where you want a natural look.

In addition to thinking about what is above ground on a tree, it's helpful to consider what will be below the ground surface as well. Some species' root systems can heave sidewalks or crack house foundations, while other tree species—such as ash, beech, birch, hawthorn, horse chestnut, and linden—are well suited for planting in confined areas.

Shrubs simultaneously create a style and enhance a sense of place. Rows of closely clipped English boxwoods suggest formality and restraint, while cascading branches of yellow-belled forsythia imply informality and exuberance. Yuccas and cacti suggest the old west; lilacs and butterfly bush hint of New England or Prince Edward's Island.

SHRUBS IN THE LANDSCAPE

In a landscape, shrubs can be used to define the shape and limits of a garden, screen some objects, and focus the eye on other, pleasing features. Shrubs can visually link a house to the ground, divide a garden into separate areas, provide colorful accents, or act as a ground cover. Shrubs are used widely as foundation plants and in borders.

Foundation plants are those that are immediately adjacent to a house. To create an attractive planting, vary the size, texture, and placement of your plants, using three or four types of shrubs well-suited to your growing area to emphasize your home's most appealing features. Place low-growing shrubs under windows and tall ones at the corners of your home or in areas where a large expanse of wall needs to be softened.

(Above) Shrubs are frequently used to fill borders around a structure. Keep the scale of the home and the mature size of the plants in mind when you choose them.

Borders—compositions of plants grouped together for a pleasing effect—usually are located along the edges of a property or along a fence line. Shrub borders are composed exclusively of shrubs, and so-called mixed borders include shrubs, flowering perennials, colorful annuals, and bulbs.

(Below) Get ideas from public gardens that you can use in your own yard on a smaller scale.

Shrub borders are reliable, low-maintenance landscape features. Generally, drifts of odd numbers of plants give a border order and elegance. For example, a grouping of three hydrangeas nestled next to a mass of five forsythias provides a more solid, pleasing look than do eight different shrubs.

A mixed border, which can provide color in the garden from spring to fall, often requires more care than does an all-shrub border. The placement of shrubs in a mixed border gives the border a strong backbone and adds a visual weight to the flowering plants.

DECIDUOUS TREES AND SHRUBS

Deciduous trees and shrubs shed their leaves in autumn or winter, then leaf out again each spring, heralding longer days and the return of warm weather. The leafy growth remains throughout summer, until autumn arrives once again. With cooling temperatures and fewer hours of sunlight, many deciduous plants put on a brilliant show with their leaves turning amber, orange, red, or yellow.

This natural cycle can be an asset. In the summer deciduous trees provide cooling shade, while in winter they allow sunlight to pass easily between their branches. When deciding on a deciduous shade tree, remember that the degree of shade provided varies considerably from species to species. Tulip trees and lindens offer fairly large amounts of shade, which is a positive feature if you live in a warm climate or if you enjoy gardening with shade-loving perennials and bulbs. On the other hand, catalpas and honey locusts allow more light to pass through their foliage, making for dappled light underneath their branches, even in midday. With these trees, you can likely grow a wider variety of flowering plants nearby.

In regions with cool climates, deciduous trees and shrubs provide autumn color. As days shorten and temperatures drop, the energy-making chlorophyll that turns leaves green begins to wane. The yellow and orange pigments that have been hidden in the leaves come to the fore, and chemical processes that create red pigments go into high gear. The results, as artists and children know, are spectacular.

If autumn foliage color is important to you, ask your local extension agent or inquire at a nursery or garden center to determine which plants produce the best color in your area. Since temperature, light, and water supply all influence the degree and duration of autumn foliage color, plants perform differently in various climates. Also take the time to select plants that exhibit the colors you want. The 'October Glory' red maple has rich reddish purple leaves in autumn, while the 'Red Sunset' maple has bright orange red foliage.

After their leafy, summer covers are shed in autumn, many deciduous trees and shrubs reveal their interesting structural forms. Contorted filbert, *Corylus avellana* 'Contorta', is one such plant. Its curiously twisted, corkscrew-like branches are a conversation piece in any garden.

(Top to bottom) Part of the glory of deciduous plants is their everchanging appearance. They flower, bear fruit, change color in autumn, and keep their charm while bare in winter.

Evergreens are plants that keep their foliage throughout the year, even in winter. They have many uses in a landscape, from serving as hedges, foundation plants, and windbreaks to providing year-round structure, definition, and beauty to a garden. Especially in cold-winter climates, they are prized for adding a touch of color to an otherwise bare winter landscape.

The two primary divisions of evergreens are needle-leaved and broad-leaved. Needle-leaved evergreens are often referred to as conifers, since most are cone-bearing plants with needlelike or scalelike leaves. (Bald cypress, larch, and dawn redwood are exceptions—they are conifers that are deciduous, shedding their needles in winter.) Conifers range in size from the coast redwood, *Sequoia sempervirens*, which grows to more than 360 feet (110 m) in height, to dwarf conifers that grow to only a few inches or centimeters tall. Cedars, firs, junipers, pines, and spruces are all conifers, and all are popular species that have multiple uses in the landscape.

Because of the wide gradations of color, size, and shape among conifers, it is possible to design a four-season garden full of contrast with these trees alone. Needle colors range from frosty silver to muted green to soft steel blue to golden yellow.

Broad-leaved evergreens have leaves rather than needles. The southern magnolia, with its large glossy leaves and intensely fragrant white blooms, is one of the most easily recognized evergreen trees. Most rhododendrons, which sport flowers in a wide range of colors in spring or summer, are among the most beloved broad-leaved evergreen shrubs.

Note that some plants may be evergreen in some climates and deciduous in others. For example, a plant such as privet might hold its leaves year-round in a very warm climate, but may shed its leaves in cold-winter areas only to releaf each spring. Similarly, some plant groups have both evergreen and deciduous members. Hollies, which are all members of the genus *Ilex*, are commonly thought of as evergreens, since most hollies hold their leaves year-round. However, there are some deciduous hollies such as *Ilex verticillata* 'Sparkleberry' and 'Winter Red', which are especially prized for their multitude of bright winter berries.

EVERGREEN TREES AND SHRUBS

Evergreens change their emphasis with the seasons. In winter (left), they are featured plants because they retain their foliage; for the rest of the year (below), they become more subdued as they mingle with deciduous plants.

SEASONAL LANDSCAPE COLOR

Color can be one of the most attractive and evocative aspects of garden design. In designing with color, a few rules of thumb are useful guides. When planning for color, keep in mind what is most suitable to your climate and to the architecture of your home. Subtle, soft color schemes are usually best for traditional homes in temperate and cool climates, since soft colors show up well in the weakened sunlight of these latitudes. In contrast, a tropical climate garden often works well with bright, vivid hues. These bright hues stand up well to the sun's glare.

If you'll be using a tree with colorful blooms as a specimen plant near your entry, or if you're planning a foundation planting of blooming shrubs, the only real consideration will be whether the bloom color looks pleasing next to your home. For a red brick home, white-flowering plants are always an excellent choice, while a white house is usually best accented by a brighter color scheme.

For trees and shrubs to be used in a mixed border, color planning requires more care. Here, an artist's color wheel might be helpful. Colors that appear opposite each other on the wheel—yellow and purple, orange and blue, green and red—are called complementary colors; they provide dramatic contrast when placed next to each other in the garden. Colors that are adjacent to one another on the wheel—such as golds, oranges, and yellows—are known as harmonizing colors. These colors blend together, giving a garden area a soothing sense of visual unity.

Keep in mind that garden color comes from foliage as well as from flowers. The leaves of shrubs and trees appear in an array of hues and shades in addition to greens. Bronze, burgundy, gold, purple, silver, and yellow are just a few of the colors that tinge foliage from early spring through late autumn. Gardeners have long used the lasting beauty of foliage color to brilliant effect. Golden plants brighten shady corners while burgundy foliage will contrast with foliage and accent a border.

COLOR TIPS

Red, orange, and yellow are warm colors. They attract attention, bring excitement and energy to a garden, and work well as focal points and accents.

Blue, purple, violet, and soft pink are cool colors. These colors make a small area appear larger, and they lend a sense of tranquillity to a garden.

Contrasting colors add drama to a landscape, while harmonizing colors create unity.

Sunlight and shade affect color perception: a white flower in deep shade may register darker than a red flower in bright sun.

Whether providing a red contrast with the snows of winter (top), fire-red fruit and green foliage in summer (middle), or the medley of color that defines autumn, trees and shrubs are stellar players in the landscape.

Once you've decided on the color scheme for your landscape and begin to select plants to carry it out, there are several factors you'll want to keep in mind so your choices will bring maximum enjoyment. In addition to bloom color, consider the

plant's bloom time, the amount of sun exposure required for the plant to flower, and the appearance of the plant when it is out of bloom.

If you enjoy your garden most in the spring and autumn, select trees and shrubs that will flower in these seasons. Conversely, if summer is when you spend most of your time outdoors, you'll want to lean heavily toward summer-bloomers. You'll find estimates of bloom times on plant tags and in encyclopedias [see Encyclopedia of Landscape Trees & Shrubs, pg. 89]. In addition, you should supplement this information with local knowledge. Talk with local extension agents or nursery staff, and make your own observations of bloom times. Because climates vary so widely, a plant that blooms in winter in one region may bloom in late spring in another part of the country. An azalea that blooms in February in Florida, for example, may bloom in April in Vancouver or May in Virginia.

Before selecting any tree or shrub for its bloom, be sure to note the plant's sun and light requirements, which also usually are given on

plant tags. While some trees and shrubs bloom well in shade, others flower most abundantly when they receive full sun. Match each plant's needs with your site's characteristics to achieve the best effect.

Finally, since bloom color is ephemeral while foliage is long-lasting, you'll want to make sure that you select trees and shrubs that will be as attractive when they are out of flower as when they are in full bloom. Study the shape, texture, color, and overall quality of the foliage of each tree or shrub you are considering. When you find the foliage that meets your needs, you're set. Numerous foliage plants are offered; continue looking until you find plants with the bloom season and exact color, as well as all of the foliage characteristics you are seeking.

FLOWERING LANDSCAPE PLANTS

(Left) Crape myrtle is a showy South African native that blooms in midsummer in areas with mild-winter climates.

(Below and inset) Lilac has long been a favorite for its fragrant, clustered blossoms that are ideal for cutting; it contrasts nicely with the simple white blooms of a flowering tree.

DESIGNING WITH TEXTURE AND SHAPE

To give a garden depth and refinement, carefully orchestrate how plant textures and shapes are used. If you follow some basic principles as you lay out your plantings, you'll create a garden that is satisfying both up close and at a distance.

When gardeners refer to the texture of a plant, they are talking about its foliage—whether it's smooth to touch or rough, glossy or dull, fuzzy or prickly. In a more general sense, plants are often classified as having fine-, medium-, or coarse-textured foliage. Needle-leaved evergreens such as hemlock and small-leaved shrubs such as heavenly bamboo are fine textured. In contrast, plants with large leaves such as southern magnolia and Japanese fatsia are considered coarse textured. While fine-textured plants have a delicate appearance, coarse-textured plants have a bolder look; medium-textured plants fall somewhere between the two.

By carefully selecting and placing plants in your garden based on their foliage texture, it is possible to create an optical illusion. Since coarse textures appear to be closer than they really are, while fine textures seem farther away, you can make a small backyard appear more expansive by putting coarsely textured plants in the foreground and gradually tapering to very finely textured shrubs at the property's edge.

You can also lend a pleasing vitality to your garden by artfully mixing textures. Place a bold-leaved shrub next to a delicate fern to accentuate the contrasting aspects of each. Similarly, if you use plants of several different shapes, your garden

(Above and inset) Foliage texture ranges from the delicate filigree of Japanese maple leaves in a group pattern to the sharp, distinctive, individual leaves found on an American holly.

(Right and inset) Exfoliating bark is common to many trees, ranging from the papery sheath of madrone (top) to the shield-like bark of sycamore.

will be visually satisfying. Plants can be as rounded as a beach ball or as columnar as an exclamation mark. They can be fountainlike or spreading, billowing or bunched. What is important is to play these shapes off one another to create dynamic compositions.

Before you plant, try different placements of your shrubs and trees while they still are in their nursery containers. Once you are satisfied with the appearance and have them where they should be placed, take

another look at the arrangement from all angles in the garden as well as from vantage points on the street and in your home. Move the plants around as necessary to get just the arrangement you want. Keep in mind their mature size, and avoid planting them too close together, too near structures, or under utility lines. Finally, when you're satisfied with the layout, then it is time to plant.

Specialty plantings include distinctive details that mark your home as being uniquely yours. Perhaps you have fond memories of playing in a treehouse as a child and you would like your own children or grandchildren to have similar memories. By planting a maple or a hickory in your backyard, you can turn that dream into a reality. If your dreams turn more toward art museums, you might want to carve out a place in your landscape to highlight a favorite garden sculpture. An evergreen hedge makes a wonderful backdrop for either a classically styled sculptural figure or an abstract art piece. Either way, the sculpture you choose and your placement of it in the garden will reflect your personal style and make the garden a more personal, intimate space.

SPECIAL AND UNIQUE PLANTINGS

WATER-WISE GARDENING

Fifty percent of the water used by homeowners is for landscape irrigation and, of that amount, nearly half is wasted. But you can design a garden to reduce water consumption and still have a lush and beautiful yard. The key is to plant in watering zones: drought-tolerant zones should contain tough plants that, once established, can thrive on the rainfall provided by nature alone; mid-level zones should consist of plants that require occasional supplemental watering during dry spells; and oasis zones should include colorful plants or specimen shrubs that need more consistent moisture.

Practically speaking, specialty plantings can make your site quieter and more sheltered. If a nearby street creates traffic noise that is noticeable in your garden, you can plant a sound-softening hedge between your home and the street. When planning the hedge, remember that broad-leaved evergreens with large cup-shaped leaves block noise more effectively than do needle-leaved conifers. The hedge should be as close to the sound source as possible, and gaps of empty air space between the trees and shrubs increase the hedge's effectiveness as a sound barrier.

If you live in a region where there are strong cold winds, you can plant a hedgerow of trees as a barrier to keep your garden or home sheltered and warm. As a rule of thumb, a row of trees gives wind protection for a distance behind the row 5–10 times its height. For example, you would have to plant a hedgerow that is 10 feet (3 m) high to protect an area that is 50–100 feet (15–30 m) deep. In addition, the row should extend as much as 50 feet (15 m) beyond the protected area on each side. This may seem like more than you need at first glance, but on blustery winter nights, you'll be thankful for the trees' sheltering properties. On calmer days the rustle of the leaves will create a soothing effect.

A creative spirit exists behind the intricate and sinuous knotted plantings seen below. Designing a feature with unusual plantings will make a distinctive statement.

ANALYZING YOUR SITE

As you get closer to planting time, it's important to analyze your site in terms of sun and wind exposure, soil type, and moisture level.

If you have a magnetic compass, you can easily note North, South, East, and West. Otherwise, carefully note where the sun rises and sets. Keep in mind that in the northern hemisphere, the summer sun rises in the northeast, traverses a high arc, and sets to the northwest, whereas the winter sun rises in the southeast, crosses low across the southern sky, and sets in the southwest; southern hemisphere gardens reverse these seasonal patterns. When it comes time to plant, you can put this type of directional knowledge to good use. For example, certain plants will flourish in sunny exposures, while others prefer cooler temperatures and shadier spots.

If you note the sun angles over a period of time, you'll see how summer and winter shadows differ. Winter shadows are longer and change more quickly. For instance, a fence that is 8 feet (2.4 m) tall might cast a shadow of 4 feet (1.2 m) in the summer but a shadow of 12 feet (3.7 m) in midwinter—a factor you'll want to keep in mind when planting trees and shrubs nearby.

While you're outside, also evaluate the type of shade your site receives. Full sun is usually defined as a minimum of 6 hours of direct sunlight per day, while full shade means an area that gets less than 2 hours of direct sun per day. An area that receives 2–5 hours of direct sun is said to be either part shade or part sun.

(Above) Most trees and shrubs grow best in sites with at least 6 hours of direct sunlight daily. Partially shaded areas should be reserved for plants that prefer low-light conditions, while plantings in hot and arid climates may need partial shade in the middle of the day.

(Right) Keep the mature size of trees in mind when planning plantings for small-space areas, and choose deep-rooted plants for areas near paving.

Moving down to ground level, inspect your soil. Dig down in several areas of your site and examine the soil to determine if it is clay, sand, or loam, and collect a soil sample to determine the soil's fertility and acidity [see Testing Soil, next pg.]. Finally, note the moisture levels in the soil by digging down several inches and feeling for dampness; repeat this over a period of time. Even if you live in an especially arid region or an area known for its rain, this is a worthwhile exercise. Moisture levels in soil differ because of variations in soil type, sun exposure, drainage issues, and other factors, so there will probably be some variation within your site, regardless of its size or location.

TREES AND SHRUBS FOR WET SITES

Trees
Bald cypress (*Taxodium distichum*)
Dawn redwood (*Metasequoia glyptostroboides*)
River birch (*Betula nigra*)
Tupelo (*Nyssa sylvatica*)
Willow (*Salix* sp.)

Shrubs
Leucothoe (*Leucothoe fontanesiana*)
Sweet pepperbush (*Clethra alnifolia*)
Sweet shrub (*Calycanthus* sp.)
Virginia sweetspire (*Itea virginica*)
Witch hazel (*Hamamelis* sp.)

TREES AND SHRUBS FOR DRY SITES

Trees
Ginkgo (*Ginkgo biloba*)
Juniper (*Juniperus* sp.)
Mesquite (*Prosopis glandulosa*)
Oak (*Quercus* sp.)
Redbud (*Cercis canadensis*)

Shrubs
Barberry (*Berberis* sp.)
Bottlebrush (*Callistemon* sp.)
Broom (*Cytisus* sp.)
Cinquefoil (*Potentilla* sp.)
Firethorn (*Pyracantha* sp.)
Manzanita (*Arctostaphylos* sp.)
Oleander (*Nerium* sp.)
Rock rose (*Cistus* sp.)

TESTING SOIL

1 Dig a hole 12 in. (30 cm) wide and deep. Using a clean trowel and plastic cup, scrape a cup (235 ml) of soil from the side of the hole, 6–8 in. (15–20 cm) from the surface. To get a representative sample, mix soil from different sections of your planting area.

Soil testing is an easy way to determine your soil's nutritional needs and acid-alkaline balance, or pH. The best garden soils are nearly equal mixtures of clay, silt, sand, and organic materials—called "loam"—and have adequate nitrogen, phosphorus, and potassium for plant growth. Most trees prefer neutral to slightly acidic soil, 6.0–7.0 pH, though some tolerate more alkaline or acidic conditions. Use a shovel, trowel, plastic cup, and soil test kit, available at garden centers and nurseries, or collect your sample for testing at a soil laboratory, following these steps:

2 Scrape a second soil sample into your hand, clenching it in your fist into a ball. When you open your hand, the soil should crumble loosely. Wet, sticky soil contains too much clay; a ball that completely falls apart indicates too-sandy soil.

3 If you're using a home test kit, read completely its instructions and follow them exactly to measure and interpret results. Mix your soil samples with distilled water, available in grocery stores. Avoid tap water.

4 For testing at a laboratory, put the soil sample into a clean plastic bag. Seal the bag and label it with your name, address, and the date of collection.

5 Wrap and send the soil sample to the laboratory. The location of soil laboratories may be obtained at garden stores, nurseries, and USDA and Agriculture Canada extensions.

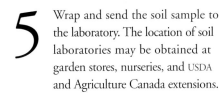

DESIGNING A LANDSCAPE

Think of your landscape as a canvas on which you are going to create a three-dimensional painting. The garden plan you will develop will be your sketch pad, on which you experiment with different designs until you find the one that suits you just right [see Creating a Garden Plan, next pg.].

In addition to creating your garden plan, which will give you a bird's-eye view of your landscape, you may also find it useful to take snapshots of your garden. After taking photographs of various aspects of your yard—the view from the street, the view from the back door looking out, the view from the driveway—enlarge the pictures on a photocopier. You can then draw on the photocopies with colored pencils, trying out different planting schemes. Imagine, for instance, that you are designing foundation plantings for your home. You can see exactly what a columnar evergreen would look like at the corner of your house, as opposed to a rounded shrub, without taking a shovel in your hands.

As you begin to sketch out your garden plan, keep in mind the landscape design principles of unity and scale [see Landscape Design: Unity, Scale, and Shape, pg. 15]. Also remember that formal homes are complemented by formal, symmetrical garden designs, while rustic homes are enhanced by looser, more naturalistic garden designs. Consistent use of curves in bed lines, walkways, and driveways can be a unifying design element and can give flow or continuity to a garden. Repeated use of right angles and straight sight lines also can be a unifying theme.

When possible, add an element of mystery to your garden by keeping one or two items out of easy view. A curving path might lead to a garden bench tucked behind a mass of hydrangeas—a miniature retreat that is all the more pleasant because it is hidden. In a small setting, consider hanging a set of wind chimes around a corner. Hearing the chimes' pleasant harmonies without seeing the source of the sound will intrigue visitors to your garden and magically make your space seem larger than it really is.

(Inset) Fixtures and features add to the ambience of many garden landscapes. Choose from fountains, gazing balls, statuary, and sundials to achieve your goal.

(Bottom) Select outdoor furniture with appearance and durability in mind. A teak bench will weather attractively and last for many years.

CREATING A GARDEN PLAN

1 Using a tape measure, stakes, and string, note the dimensions of the outside perimeter of your garden area. Measure each curve as a segment of a circle with a measured radius.

A garden plan—sometimes called a "base plan"—is a scale diagram of your landscaped yard. Two things must be done for an accurate plan: careful measurements are taken, then those measurements are transferred to paper or a computer equipped with design software. If you choose to automate the process, follow the instructions of the software producer for best results. Here, the traditional process is used, following these steps:

2 Using two fixed points such as corners of the area, measure the distance to each structure or existing element.

3 Repeat by measuring to utilities and trees, shrubs, or other greenery that you plan to keep in your landscape or garden.

4 On graph paper, using a straightedge ruler, compass, and pencils, construct a scale diagram of the garden perimeter. Scales of ¼ in. to 1 ft. (5 mm to 30 cm) are commonly used.

6 Complete your garden plan by noting North and the other cardinal directions on the margin of the diagram.

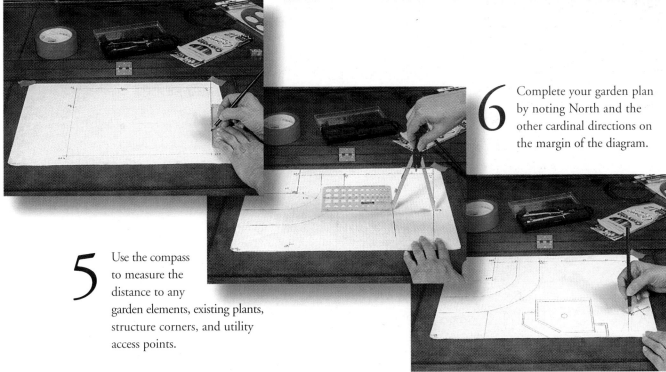

5 Use the compass to measure the distance to any garden elements, existing plants, structure corners, and utility access points.

SELECTING LANDSCAPE PLANTS

(Right) Go beyond green when choosing foliage shrubs for your landscape. Both evergreens and deciduous plants bear distinctive blue, pink, and yellow foliage.

(Below) During its season of dormancy, birch adds beauty to the landscape with its bark, and cones provide seed to passing birds.

With garden plan in hand, you can select the trees and shrubs that will turn your drawing into a living reality. First learn as much as you can about your options, then choose plants based on the landscape function you want them to fulfill, each plant's adaptability to your site's climate, soil type, and sun exposures, and the degree of maintenance each will need to keep it healthy and attractive. Other factors that come into play during the selection process are the looks of the plant and—in some cases—the plant's ability to attract birds and butterflies.

To learn about your options, turn to plant encyclopedias such as the one included in this book [see Encyclopedia of Landscape Trees & Shrubs, pg. 89]. These lists are packed with information on the needs of each featured plant. Some of the same information often is noted on plant tags as well. Details such as the tree or shrub's mature size, and whether it is deciduous or evergreen, will help you determine if it is suitable for your landscape's site and purpose.

One of the first considerations is whether the plant is adapted to your cold hardiness zone [see USDA Plant Hardiness Around the World, pg. 132]. Also note the plant's needs in terms of soil, light, and water. Some plants are very specific in their needs, while others are adaptable to a wide range of conditions.

Once you've studied a plant's cultural requirements, assess its visual impact. Attractive foliage, pretty flowers, distinctive branching habits, and brightly colored fruit are bold accents. As a final criterion, you may want to select plants based on their attractiveness to birds or butterflies. This information is sometimes indicated on plant tags and in plant encyclopedias, and also can be found in lists published by groups such as the National Wildlife Federation in the United States and the Canadian Wildlife Federation.

CREATING LAYERED LANDSCAPES

Layered plantings contain mixed overstory trees, midheight shrubs, low-growing plants, and ground cover. Planning layers starts by choosing trees and shrubs [see Encyclopedia of Landscape Trees & Shrubs, pg. 89]. A layered elevation sketch will help you visualize the landscape you are planning. Gather a scaling ruler, tracing paper, colored pencils, and an eraser, then follow these steps:

1 On tracing paper, draw a baseline equal in length to the garden width. Mark the scale location of each landscape tree you will plant.

2 Mature trees have distinctive forms. Estimate the mature height and width of the first tree, then scale them on the diagram. With a dark green pencil, sketch and fill in an outline of each tree you'll plant.

3 Overlay your tree diagram with a second layer of tracing paper. Repeat the process, sketching the location and height of each shrub planned for the garden, filling it with medium green.

4 On a third overlay, repeat the process for your lower-growing shrubs and ground covers. Fill them in with two shades of light green.

5 Working backwards through the layers with fresh tracing paper, copy the foreground shrubs first, then the midheight shrubs, then the trees, creating a realistic profile of your layered landscape.

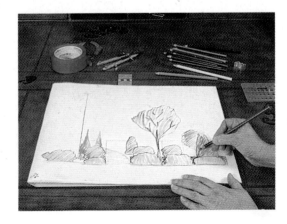

SPACING TREES AND SHRUBS

Proper spacing of trees and shrubs is important for many reasons—so plants can grow to their natural form; to allow for good air circulation, which is essential for keeping plants healthy; to give plants adequate access to nutrients and sunlight; and to avoid excessive pruning in future years.

Spacing recommendations are usually based on the mature width of a plant. If an azalea will grow 4 feet (1.2 m) wide, in most cases you'll want to plant a group of azaleas 4 feet (1.2 m) apart so that they will just touch at maturity. Even if your planting looks sparse initially, in a few years the azaleas will fill out and make a beautiful statement.

If you are planting two different species next to each other, you can split the recommended planting distance. For example, if one shrub reaches 12 feet (3.7 m) at maturity and another shrub reaches 6 feet (1.8 m), plant them 9 feet (2.7 m) apart. In the case of hedge plantings, you may want to plant shrubs a little more closely together than recommended so that a solid screen will quickly develop.

When putting in foundation plantings, be sure that even at maturity there will be enough room to walk comfortably between the plants and your home. This maintenance zone will allow you to paint the house or perform other household repairs, or to routinely reach water faucets and hoses.

(Above) Choose plants that will avoid future challenges. Shallow-rooted, invasive trees can lift pavement and increase the effort needed to mow beneath them, while others can interfere with overhead utility lines.

(Far right) Features such as in-ground pools should be protected when you plant nearby. Allow the recommended spacing for the species, plus an extra safety factor of 50 percent more.

(Right) Marking paint or flour will help you visualize the mature spread of your plantings.

Near a sidewalk or other walkway, give plants enough of a setback that pedestrians will be able to walk by easily. If a tree or shrub will be near a driveway, be sure that clear sight lines will remain even at the plant's maturity, so cars can safely enter and exit.

Remember plants' heights as well. Make sure to plant trees far enough away from power lines and telephone wires so their limbs can grow freely without becoming entangled in the lines. If you are planting near driveways or side-walks, select vase-shaped trees with ascending branches such as the Japanese zelkova, which will allow easy passage underneath.

Consider your neighbors as you position your plants. A tree planted near your property line eventually may have limbs and roots that extend into their yard. Select species that are suitable for the space, and check with your neighbors before you plant.

PLANNING A TREE AND SHRUB BORDER

1 Secure your base diagram beneath a tracing-paper overlay. On the overlay, draw a diagram of the area that will be the bed.

Borders are landscape features that follow existing structures such as dwellings, fences, paths, and streets. Usually narrow and long, they look best when planted with permanent trees and shrubs. Often, planting areas are included for annual and perennial bedding plants. Gather your garden plan, tracing paper, scaling ruler, and colored pencils, then follow these steps:

2 Note with dotted lines areas of shade cast across the bed by nearby structures or existing trees. Remember that shadows change as the day passes.

3 Mark the planting location of each tree at half its recommended spacing from other trees and any structures. Keeping scale in mind, draw a circle depicting each tree's mature width.

4 On a second tissue overlay, estimate the shade areas cast by the new trees using dotted lines and colored pencil. Note where full-sun, partial-sun, and shady sites exist in the planting bed.

6 Add a legend with the species, variety, and quantity needed for each plant. Make a photocopy of the finished plan to consult when picking plants.

5 Place the tissue between the base diagram and your planting plan. Mark the planting location of each shrub, then draw circles depicting their mature spread.

Y

ou've analyzed your site, turned your dreams and desires into a garden plan, and selected your shrubs and trees. Now you are ready to head into the garden and plant. But before you rush out, take the time to read this chapter. You'll learn all about the most up-to-date planting techniques.

If you're planting in containers, you'll see how to select planters, how to choose the best planting soil, and how to plant your container trees and shrubs to get them off to a good start. If your garden plan includes planting shrubs in landscape beds, you'll find out how to lay out a bed and amend the soil. Once the bed is ready, you'll learn step-by-step how to dig planting holes and put the shrubs in the ground.

You'll find information about the latest recommended methods of planting trees. Scientific research shows that newly planted trees do best when the soil in the planting hole matches the surrounding soil. This means holding back on amendments and using only the native soil as backfill. The new method is more effective than was the traditional technique of adding amendments to the soil in the planting hole, and it will reduce the effort involved as well as conserve your resources. You'll also learn that the size and depth of the planting hole you'll need to dig is important to helping the plant adjust to its new surroundings.

Once your trees and shrubs are in the ground, proper care of your plants will help your garden develop and grow. You'll learn how to water and care for young plants, how to stake vulnerable young trees, and how to transplant established trees and shrubs if necessary to accomplish your goals.

As you begin the exciting task of putting your plants into the ground, remember that the proper planting techniques will ensure a healthy start for your trees and shrubs and will accrue benefits in years to come. A tree or shrub that has been well selected and well planted will bring you years of joy and will likely live on for future generations to admire and enjoy.

A guide to soil conditioning, installing beds, and caring for your new trees and shrubs

Preparing and Planting

Landscaping a new home means planting many shrubs and trees. It's your choice whether to divide the task into sections, or to plant everything at the same time.

SHRUBS AND TREES IN CONTAINERS

Choosing the right planter for your tree or shrub is the first step to a successful container planting. Good drainage is essential for healthy plants, so make sure that your container has an adequate number of drainage holes. If you have your heart set on an unusual planter that lacks holes, in most cases you can drill some yourself.

Concrete, plastic, stone, terra cotta, and wood are all good options for container materials. If you live in a cold-winter climate, you'll want to use containers that can withstand freezing temperatures. In this case, the best choices are high-quality wood planters, thick stone planters, or the new lightweight containers made from fiberglass, polyethylene, or structural foam. The latter are often molded to resemble terra cotta or concrete, and can be quite handsome.

With trees and shrubs, often the size of the container will be an issue. Large planters offer better support for plants with extensive root systems, since they can hold a greater volume of soil, water, and nutrients. But once planted and watered, large pots can be very heavy. Place containers in their permanent location prior to planting, or set them on roll-about dollies so that they easily can be moved.

(Right) Structural containers help emphasize specimen trees. They generally are built with masonary blocks and open bottoms that allow the trees to root into the native soil.

(Below) Use concrete or other heavy planters for container trees that will grow tall to protect them from tipping in the wind.

As a planting medium, choose a high-quality potting soil made specifically for each container plant. While nurseries and garden centers stock both soil-based and lightweight soil-free potting mixes, it's a good idea to choose a soil-based mix if you are planting a large-sized tree or shrub. These heavier mixes will help anchor the plant's root system and provide a sturdier base if the plant is exposed to high winds.

If you are planting water-loving plants such as hydrangeas, you may want to consider adding water-retaining polymers, commonly called "hydrogels," to the planting mix. These polymers bind water molecules when moist, then they slowly release the water into the surrounding soil as it dries. For plants such as cacti that require arid conditions, using a potting soil that will dry thoroughly between waterings is necessary.

PLANTING INTO DECORATIVE CONTAINERS

For container shrubs and trees, it's best to choose species that are slow growing or naturally dwarfed. Remember that large containers filled with soil are heavy; it's a good idea to plant them at the location where they will be displayed. Always set the container on pot feet to allow proper drainage. Gather a large container, filter fabric, pea gravel, a hand trowel, ruler, potting soil, your tree or shrub, and a watering can, then follow these simple planting steps:

1 Prevent the pot's drain hole from clogging by lining the container base with porous filter fabric and pea gravel, 2–3 in. (50–75 mm) thick.

2 Measure from the nursery container's base to the soil's surface. Fill the planting pot's base with soil until its remaining space equals the depth of the nursery container.

3 Lay the plant on its side. Slowly roll it as you press and release the sides to loosen the rootball. Hold the trunk or stem at its base, then gently push on the container to free the plant.

4 Unwind or cut any encircling roots with a trowel or knife. Score the sides of the rootball.

5 With a helper, grasp the rootball and settle the plant into the new container. Fill around the roots with soil.

6 Thoroughly water the plant and allow it to drain. Add soil if any uneven settling occurs.

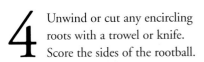

RAISED BEDS AND BERMS

Planting beds for shrubs and small trees can be at ground level, or they can be above ground level. You can use raised beds to add interest to a flat site or to improve drainage in poorly drained areas. In areas of poor soil, raised beds filled with good topsoil can provide an excellent base for plants that might otherwise be difficult to grow.

Traditional raised beds usually have stones, bricks, railroad ties, planking, or other hardscape materials built around them to hold the bed's soil in place. Choose your materials to complement the style of your home. They can be formal and geometric in shape, or they can be more loosely configured. Berms are similar to traditional raised beds, but instead of having walls to hold the soil in place, the soil slopes down to ground level. Berms are excellent for contouring a garden, and they have a very natural appearance.

Regardless of the type of bed you are preparing, you can lay out the shape of the bed using a flexible garden hose or rope. Move the hose around until you have the size and shape exactly to your liking—it can be round, sinuous, or rectangular. Once you're satisfied, mark the outline with flour or stakes. To build a traditional raised bed, follow the steps shown on the next page. In most cases additional topsoil will be needed to fill the bed. If the planting bed will be raised 12 inches (30 cm) or more off the ground, work the topsoil into the native soil to a depth of about 6 inches (15 cm). For lower beds, mix the new soil with your native soil to a depth of at least 12 inches (30 cm).

IN-GROUND IRRIGATION

With in-ground irrigation, keeping your plants watered becomes almost effortless. And because an irrigation system makes it so convenient to water, you're more likely to give your plants the right amount of water at the right time of day, so that they stay healthy.

Installing an irrigation system is detailed later in this book [see Installing an Automatic Deep-Watering System, pg. 77]. If you are building a raised bed, the best time to place the supply lines is now, during construction.

(Above) Raised beds are the best choice for formal plantings such as this rose garden. As you see in the construction photograph, each planter has its own water supply for irrigation of the shrubs.

(Right) Raised landscape beds are the answer for large tree and shrub groups.

(Inset) An in-ground island bed set off with a neat hedge requires the least effort to install. It' a good option for gardens that include shrubs of varied heights.

BUILDING A RAISED SHRUB BED

1 Measure and mark the outline of the planter with flour or marking paint, then excavate trench footings 8 in. (20 cm) deep.

Railroad ties and galvanized pipe make strong, durable, structural landscape planters that are ideal for shrub borders. Pipes pin the timbers together and anchor the planter to the subsurface soil. To build your planter, gather a reciprocating saw, electric drill, spade bit, ties, landscape fabric, pipe, shovel, flour, pea gravel, and a sledge hammer, then follow these steps:

2 Line the footing trench with landscape fabric to prevent roots from penetrating the structure, then add a layer of pea gravel to the trench, 4 in. (10 cm) deep.

3 Lay a first course of timbers, overlapping them to create flush corners. Using a power drill that is fitted with a ⅞-in. (22-mm) spade bit, drill holes vertically, 8 in. (20 cm) from each end of the timbers.

4 Lay a second course of timbers, overlapping them, log-cabin fashion, to avoid aligning joints. Mark and drill through the timbers to join with the first course's holes.

5 Temporarily install a threaded end cap on a length of ½-in. (12-mm) galvanized pipe, 32 in. (80 cm) long. Using a sledge-hammer, drive it through the aligned holes and into the soil underlaying the bed.

6 Remove the end cap, and use the sledge hammer to drive the pipe flush with the timber. Repeat at each pair of holes. Fill the bed with soil.

AMENDING AND FERTILIZING SOIL

Depending on your site's soil type, you may want to amend your soil by adding organic matter to it before planting your shrubs. Amendments enrich the soil and improve the soil's tilth—its physical structure. You can use any type of organic matter—compost, composted animal manures, decomposed bark, or leaf mold.

Both clay and sandy soils can be improved by tilling in compost or well-rotted manures. In clay soils, these amendments improve drainage and aeration, while they increase sandy soils' moisture-holding capabilities. In both cases, the amendments increase the activity of beneficial microorganisms and improve the soil's ability to hold and release nutrients [see Site and Soil, pg. 12].

Some amendments also adjust pH levels. Add dolomitic limestone to highly acidic soil to raise its pH, or work sulfur into highly alkaline soils to lower the pH. In both cases, base the amount of limestone or sulfur you add on the recommendations provided by soil test results [see Testing Soil, pg. 33].

A side benefit of organic amendments is that they provide trace amounts of micro-nutrients and trace elements to the soil. The three key nutrients for plants are nitrogen, phosphorus, and potassium. They need nitrogen for foliage growth, phosphorus for root growth and flower development, and potassium to make them more winter-hardy and drought tolerant. Most soils contain these nutrients in sufficient amounts, but if a soil test indicates that your soil is deficient in one or more of them, you'll want to add an appropriate fertilizer to the planting bed.

A fertilizer's analysis is shown on its label, displayed as three numbers (for example, 10–10–10, 0–5–5, or 15–1–1). The first number refers to the percentage of nitrogen (N) that's contained in the fertilizer, the second number to the percentage of phosphorus (P), and the third number to the percentage of potassium (K). In accordance with your soil test results, select the fertilizer that matches your needs. If you're uncertain, select a slow-release, low-potency, balanced fertilizer and use it sparingly in your planting beds, mixing it deeply and thoroughly into the soil.

(Above) An electronic moisture meter will help you decide when the soil has dried and needs watering.

(Right) Garden tillers are helpful for mixing soil amendments and fertilizers. Keep in mind that their tines reach only a few inches into the soil and, for better mixing, you should double-dig the bed.

(Below) Amendments improve the texture or change the acid-alkaline balance of soil, while fertilizers add nutrients. Compost is both a light fertilizer and a texture enhancer. Garden lime and sulfur are used to alter pH.

PREPARING SOIL
FOR PLANTING SHRUBS

1 Begin by clearing all weeds and plants you plan to remove. Remove rocks and debris at least 18 in. (45 cm) deep.

Soil for shrub plantings should be amended and fertilized before planting; you should plant trees in native soil. Most amendments improve soil texture, adding air, retaining moisture, and hastening drainage. Fertilizers add the nutrients shrubs need to grow. Test your soil to determine what amendments and fertilizers you'll need [see Testing Soil, pg. 33]. Gather rakes, shovel or spading fork, a tarp, tiller, wheelbarrow or garden cart, amendments, and fertilizer, then follow these steps:

2 Dig a trench 9–12 in. (23–30 cm) deep and one shovel width wide along an edge of the bed, placing the removed soil on a tarp. Loosen the next 9–12 in. (23–30 cm) of soil within the trench with a spading fork or shovel.

3 Widen the trench a second shovel width, placing the top 9–12 in. (23–30 cm) of its soil into the first trench. Progress across the area until all the soil has been dug. Fill the last trench with soil from the first. Use a tiller to thoroughly mix the topsoil.

4 Cover the area with a 4-in. (10-cm) layer of organic soil amendment, as needed. Add synthetic or organic fertilizer, as needed, following package instructions.

5 Turn the soil amendments into the top 9–12 in. (23–30 cm) of soil using a shovel or fork.

6 Rake the top of the bed smooth. It will be high and fluffy with air and amendments; avoid compacting it to retain its texture. Water with a sprinkler and allow it to settle for at least 24 hours before planting.

PLANTING SHRUBS AND HEDGES

Before digging planting holes, place your shrubs in their containers atop the ground in the spots where you'll plant them. Walk around and assess the arrangement—it's easier to move the shrubs before planting than to transplant them later. Look at the grouping, and then at each individual plant from every viewing angle. If the shrubs will be seen from only one side, be sure they have their best, most shapely side facing forward. Rotate each plant until it is just right, keeping in mind the recommended spacing.

(Right) Space shrub plantings at the recommended distance for the species to ensure that they will grow into a solid hedge.

(Below) Growing a hedge is the gardener's answer to fencing. It will take 3–4 seasons for the hedge to grow in, several more for it to reach final height.

If you are planting a shrub in a prepared bed, dig a hole the same depth and slightly wider than the plant's rootball. Remove the shrub from its container and untwist any encircling roots. If the rootball is matted, cut three or four slits starting at its bottom and going halfway up the side. Place the rootball in the planting hole and fan out the roots. Backfill with soil from the bed and water well.

If you are planting a shrub in an existing bed, dig a hole the same depth as the rootball but three times as wide. Using a pitchfork or other tined tool, poke holes extending from the planting hole outward into the surrounding soil—these holes will be the medium through which the plant's roots will eventually reach out. To plant a containerized or balled-and-burlapped shrub that's growing in soil similar in texture to your native soil, place the rootball in the planting hole, keeping the top of the rootball even with or slightly higher than the surrounding soil, and backfill with native soil. If your shrub is growing in soil that is of a very different texture from your native soil—for example, if the shrub is in a coarse potting soil and your native soil is clayey—then gently wash away some of the potting soil with a garden hose. Once this has been done, place the rootball in the planting hole and backfill with native soil until the hole is a third full. Water thoroughly, letting the soil settle before you finish filling the hole with the remaining native soil.

To plant a formal hedge that you want to be perfectly straight, it is helpful to sink a stake in the ground at each end and tie a string between the stakes as an alignment guide. Placing the string fairly high above the ground will keep it well out of the way of your shovel, making the job much easier.

PLANTING NURSERY CONTAINER SHRUBS

Shrubs grown in nursery containers quickly will establish themselves in prepared soil [see Preparing Soil for Planting Shrubs, pg. 47]. Because the shrubs may have been held for a time at the grower or retailer, they might be rootbound—tightly rooted in the container. Gather a shovel, gloves, and your shrubs, then follow these planting steps:

1 Use the shrub in its nursery container to gauge the size of the planting hole to dig. It should be as deep as the soil in the pot, and 3 times as wide.

2 Lay the container with the plant on its side, compressing it as you roll it back and forth. This loosens the soil and roots from the container sides.

3 Gently grasp the main stem at its base. Holding the plant, slide the container from the rootball. Avoid pulling on the plant.

4 Unwind or cut any encircling roots, including those that are on the bottom of the rootball. The plant quickly will sprout replacement roots.

5 Set the shrub into the plantng hole, then backfill around it. Tamp the soil firm using your open palms to compress it. Add additional soil if necessary.

6 Water thoroughly. Repeat the watering in 24 hours, then again a few days later. After 10 days, water weekly or as needed.

SPECIAL NEEDS OF TREES

Trees planted today will likely live for decades—perhaps even centuries. In 20 or 30 years' time, an oak sapling with a rootball 12 inches (30 cm) wide can grow to 70 feet (21 m) high and wide; since most root systems extend to three times the width of a tree's crown, that translates to a root system stretching 210 feet (64 m) in diameter.

A key to growing long-lived trees is to start with trees that are well adapted to your soil type and other site conditions [see Selecting Landscape Plants, pg. 36]. While catalpa, scarlet oak, and sassafras will thrive in clay soils, other trees, such as arborvitae, red oak, and white pine prefer sandy soils.

Another step to growing a healthy tree is to plant the young tree in soil that is similar in type and texture to the soil that its entire root system will occupy at maturity.

(Above) Care for recent plantings for at least two seasons, ensuring regular water and fertilizing.

(Right) Instant landscapes are possible through installation of large boxed specimen trees.

(Below) Tree-planting essentials include a barrow, shovel, gloves, compost, and the tree.

Assume, for example, that you are planting a shade tree and your site consists of heavy clay soil. Unless you plan to amend the entire site—at least 100 feet (30 m) in every direction—your sapling will do better in the long run if it is planted in unamended clay soil. Extensive planting research has shown that trees planted with only native soil in the planting hole develop larger, better-established root systems than those planted in holes to which amendments have been added.

In some cases, you may wish to enhance your soil by the addition of so-called mycorrhizal fungi—organisms that promote tree root development. Most healthy soils contain sufficient amounts of these fungi, but tightly compacted soil that has been compressed by construction equipment or heavy foot traffic may need supplements. Mycorrhizal cultures are available at many nurseries and from direct retailers.

If all the topsoil has been removed from your site—perhaps during the process of building your new home—and now only subsoil remains, you may want to bring in a quantity of new topsoil before you plant your trees and shrubs. You can order topsoil from many home improvement retailers, whose staff can help you calculate the proper amount.

DIGGING A TREE-PLANTING HOLE

Because it's best to plant trees directly in native soil, the planting hole should be about 2–4 in. (50–100 mm) wider than the nursery container, burlapped ball, or box. Gather a shovel, measuring tape, and gloves, and follow these steps:

1 Measure the rootball's height from its base to the soil surface. This should be the depth of the planting hole. Measure the rootball's diameter to determine the hole's width, which should be 2–4 in. (50–100 mm) wider than the container.

2 Dig the planting hole, setting excavated soil at least 3 ft. (90 cm) away from the hole's edge. You'll need full access later when you position the tree.

3 If the planting adjoins a path, driveway, or structure, install barrier fabric or sheet plastic to guard against surface roots.

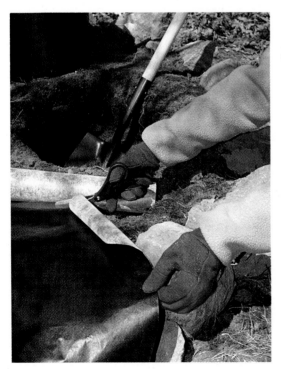

4 In arid climates or those with sandy, fast-draining soils, install a deep-watering tube at the edge of the planting hole. Block its end with landscape fabric and fill it with gravel.

PLANTING TREES

Tree-planting techniques vary slightly, depending on whether your tree is balled-and-burlapped, bare root, boxed, or in a nursery container.

When planting a containerized tree, dig a planting hole the same depth as the rootball, and 2–4 in. (50–100 mm) wider. Using a pitchfork or other tined tool, poke holes into the bottom and sides of the hole, penetrating the surrounding soil—these holes will become the outlets through which the tree roots will eventually grow. Carefully remove the tree from its container, loosen and fan out the roots, and prune any damaged roots. Place the rootball in the planting hole, making sure that the roots are relatively straight and fanned down. Be sure the top of the rootball is level with the soil or slightly higher. Backfill with native soil that has been broken up with a shovel. Gently tamp the soil as you go to remove any air pockets, but remember that you want the soil to be loose and breathable.

If your tree is growing in a potting medium that is of a different texture from your native soil, gently wash away some of the potting soil with a garden hose, then place the rootball in the planting hole. Backfill the hole with native soil until it's one-third full. Water thoroughly, let the soil settle, then finish filling the hole with the remaining native soil.

(Right top) Comply with all local codes and homeowner's covenants when you plant trees. For sites near buried utility lines, notify the utility before proceeding.

(Right) Prepare bare-root trees by soaking them in water for 24 hours prior to planting.

(Below) It's best to gather all of your materials, equipment, and plants at the site before digging begins. Water the tree the night before planting. If the site's soil is compacted, wet it thoroughly 48 hours before.

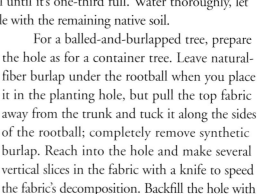

For a balled-and-burlapped tree, prepare the hole as for a container tree. Leave natural-fiber burlap under the rootball when you place it in the planting hole, but pull the top fabric away from the trunk and tuck it along the sides of the rootball; completely remove synthetic burlap. Reach into the hole and make several vertical slices in the fabric with a knife to speed the fabric's decomposition. Backfill the hole with soil and water well.

When planting a bare-root tree, soak the roots in water for several hours before planting. Dig a planting hole wide and deep enough to accommodate the roots. Make a cone-shaped mound of soil in the center of the hole, then set the roots in the hole, spreading them out over the mound. Backfill with soil until the hole is three-quarters full, and water thoroughly. Let the soil settle, then finish filling the hole with the remaining native soil and water once again.

Boxed trees are usually large specimen trees. They are planted similarly to nursery container trees, but because of their size they are often planted by tree professionals [see Planting Large Specimen Trees, pg. 55].

PLANTING BARE-ROOT TREES

Bare-root trees and shrubs are available each spring. Usually vigorous species, they quickly develop roots when planted in unamended garden soil. Gather a ruler or measuring tape, shovel, gloves, and your tree, then follow these easy steps:

1 Notice the discolored point on the trunk marking the tree's previous soil level. Measure the depth from that point to the center of the root crown's base.

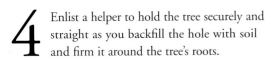

2 Dig a planting hole 4–6 in. (10–15 cm) deeper than the tree's root crown depth and half again the distance its roots' spread. Create a cone-shaped mound in its center, 4–6 in. (10–15 cm) high.

3 Place the tree in the planting hole straddling the mound and spreading the roots evenly around it. Use a shovel handle across the hole to check that the tree's depth matches that of its prior planting.

4 Enlist a helper to hold the tree securely and straight as you backfill the hole with soil and firm it around the tree's roots.

5 Raise a moat around the outer perimeter of the planting hole, 3–4 in. (75–100 mm) high, to create a watering basin.

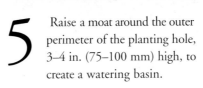

6 Thoroughly water the tree within the watering basin. Add soil if any uneven settling occurs.

PLANTING SMALL TREES

Most trees are planted either balled-and-burlapped or from nursery containers, depending on local custom. Choose fresh stock from recent arrivals for the most dependable results. Like bare roots, they should be planted in unamended garden soil. Gather a shovel, tape measure, and your tree, then follow these steps:

Balled-and-Burlapped

1 Move the tree to your planting site. Loosen the burlap's ties and measure from the soil surface to the rootball's base. Dig a hole as deep as the rootball's depth and one-third wider.

2 Untie and peel back the burlap, folding it down around the root-ball. For synthetic burlap, remove it entirely.

3 With a helper, lift the rootball and set the tree into the hole. Backfill around the tree.

4 Build a basin by raising a moat around the outer perimeter of the hole, 3–4 in. (75–100 mm) high. Water thoroughly.

Nursery Container Trees

1 Measure the depth of the soil in the nursery container. Dig a hole about 2–4 in. (50–100 mm) wider than the container and as deep as the container's soil.

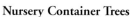

2 Lay the container on its side. Loosen the soil around the rootball, then slide the container from the tree's roots. Carefullly unwind any encircling roots.

3 Set the tree in the planting hole. Backfill with native soil, settling it with your palms. Water the tree thoroughly.

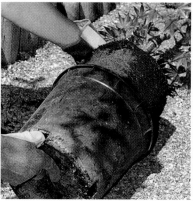

PLANTING LARGE SPECIMEN TREES

Boxed trees, sometimes of large size, have become popular for planting in residential landscapes. While very large specimen trees should be planted using the assistance of experts, trees with rootballs up to 4 ft. (1.2 m) wide can be planted with a few helpers. Gather a shovel, sturdy planks, hammer, crowbar, sheet metal shears, and your tree, then follow these steps:

1 With a helper, lay the tree on its side. Completely remove the wooden bottom of the box. The box's tapered shape will support the tree.

2 Set the tree upright. Note its best face and rotate the tree so its orientation matches the planting hole. With sheet metal shears, cut the lower binding strap.

3 With a helper, raise the side of the box nearest the hole, sliding two planks beneath it. The planks should reach beyond the box to halfway across the planting hole.

4 Using the planks as slides, push the tree over the hole. Control its descent by using the planks as levers.

5 With the tree positioned in the hole, use shears to cut the top binding strap and a crowbar to remove the box's sides. Backfill with native soil.

6 Build a dike around the tree, about the same diameter as the old box and 4–6 in. (10–15 cm) high. Water the tree extensively, adding soil to fill any uneven settling.

STAKING AND SUPPORT FOR TREES

Young trees need to move and sway in the wind to some degree in order to develop into strong and sturdy specimens. In fact, research has shown that trees that are allowed to sway naturally in the wind develop more anchor roots, produce wider trunk diameters, and develop more reaction wood—wood that withstands natural flexing—than do trees that have been rigidly staked.

In some cases, however, newly planted trees benefit from being staked. Trees with relatively thin trunks and large crowns often need support to remain upright, while trees planted in sandy soils or in windy areas may benefit from staking to stabilize them until their root systems expand adequately.

Very small trees may be supported by a single stake. In this case, place the stake on the upwind side of the tree, 8 inches (20 cm) from the trunk. It is a good idea to place the stake in the hole when you plant the tree; you may unintentionally damage the roots if you drive the stake in later. Use a soft, slightly elastic material to tie the tree to the stake in a figure-eight loop at two or more points.

Larger trees typically are supported by two or more stakes. You can install two stakes opposite each other, and then extend the ties in a horseshoe pattern [see Installing Support Stakes and Ties, next pg.]. If the tree is planted in a windy area or if its trunk is greater than 3 inches (75 mm) in diameter, it is best to use three stakes. In this case, place the stakes equidistantly around the tree, with guy wires 6 inches (15 cm) above the level where the tree trunk becomes floppy. Any parts of the staking equipment that touch the tree should be flexible and soft to prevent damage to the bark.

When you stake a tree, be sure the ties are sufficiently loose for the tree to move naturally in response to light winds—in most cases, 3–4 inches (75–100 mm) of sway is adequate. After the first growing season, you can remove any stakes and guy wires from most trees and allow them to stand on their own.

(Above) Stretchy plastic plant tape is the best choice for supporting and tying limbs. It avoids girdling the branches.

(Right) Many pit-fruit trees grow weak-crotched limbs that require support to keep them from breaking under the load of fruit. This peach tree has been braced to carry the fruits' weight.

(Below) Some woody shrubs such as firethorn bear heavy loads of berries. Plant them near a sturdy support.

INSTALLING SUPPORT STAKES AND TIES

Plant stakes are installed to support the young tree or shrub while permitting it to move. Flexing of the trunk triggers the plant to develop wood, making the stem stiff and strong. The ties are installed to permit the tree to flex over a range of motion. Gather two wooden stakes and rubber tree ties, a stake-driving tool, hammer, nails, wire cutters, and gloves, then follow these steps:

1 Set the two stakes on opposite sides of the trunk, at right angles to any prevailing wind. Use the stake driver to set each stake into the soil, about 14 in. (35 cm) from the trunk.

2 Loop a tie around the trunk, positioning it about 12 in. (30 cm) from the top of a stake. Wrap the ties' wires once around the stake, then secure it to the stake using a nail.

3 Loop a second tie around the trunk, weaving it through the other tie. Check that the trunk has 3–4 in. (75–100 mm) space to move within the ties.

4 Secure the second tie's wires to the opposite stake with a nail. Cut off any dangling wire that could pose a safety hazard. If the installed stakes are too tall, cut them to size.

TRANSPLANTING TREES AND SHRUBS

It is sometimes necessary to move established trees and shrubs from one part of the garden to another—perhaps the addition of a deck in your backyard will necessitate the moving of a small tree, or a previous homeowner planted a shrub that you'd prefer in a different location. Whatever the reason, the secret to transplanting success lies in correct timing, good technique, and ample watering after the move.

The best time to transplant trees and shrubs is generally in autumn or early winter, when deciduous plants are dormant and evergreens are in a resting state. Moving plants in the dormant season allows the plant's energy to be directed to root growth, so that by the time top growth occurs in the spring the roots will be ready to provide the water and nutrient uptake required.

Another reason it's best to transplant during the dormant season is to keep water loss through a plant's leaves to a minimum. During dormancy, deciduous plants have dropped their leaves, while evergreens' leaves continue to transpire—lose water—at a much slower pace. If you are transplanting an evergreen at any time of the year, or a deciduous plant during the growing season, consider using an antitranspirant spray. Available at most nurseries and garden centers, these sprays reduce the amount of water loss through the leaves and ease transplanting shock.

When it's time to transplant, dig a trench around the plant, aiming for as large a rootball as you can. For a spreading plant, dig at least midway between the trunk and the branch tips; for a columnar plant allow 1 foot (30 cm) in diameter of rootball for every 2 feet (60 cm) of height.

As you trench around the plant, push the shovel straight down to get as clean a cut as possible on the roots. It may help to remove some of the excess soil with a hand trowel as you dig deeper. When you have dug 1½–2 feet (45–60 cm) deep, carefully lever up the rootball, supporting it as much as possible with a broad, flat shovel.

Carefully transport the plant to its new location, using a wheelbarrow or the help of a friend if necessary. Replant as soon as you possibly can, employing the same techniques used for the planting of a new tree or shrub [see Planting Shrubs and Hedges, pg. 48, and Planting Trees, pg. 52]. Irrigate immediately, then continue to water well throughout the next growing season or until the plant is well established.

Always thoroughly water new plantings after they are finished. It accomplishes two important goals: restoring water lost from the rootball during planting, and settling the soil in the hole.

TRANSPLANTING A SMALL TREE

1 When leaves have fallen, prune the tree's outer and top seasonal growth, reducing the crown by about one-third and leaving the growth points. Also remove any low branches, and trim the small, interior twigs.

Ideally, trees should be transplanted before they have become fully established, usually within 1–5 years of first planting. Transplanting requires preparation and considerable effort, including digging and heavy lifting. You'll need shovels, picks, saws, stout timbers, gloves, and one or more helpers. Begin the transplant process in autumn, following these steps:

2 Using flour or garden lime, mark a circle around the tree directly beneath its outermost branches, at the drip line. Dig a vertical trench outside the circle, 2–3 ft. (60–90 cm) wide and 3 ft (90 cm) deep.

3 Use a saw to cut off branching roots that extend into the trench. Soil under the tree's roots should be 8–12 in. (20–30 cm) deep.

4 Working at opposite sides, undercut the tree to its center. Place timbers to support the rootball as it is freed.

5 With helpers or lifting equipment, support and raise the rootball. Wrap it with burlap before transporting it to the new planting site. Plant as you would a specimen tree.

AFTER-PLANTING CARE

Tending to your newly planted tree or shrub is important to its long-term health. One of the most important aspects of after-planting care is watering. A thorough, slow watering of trees and shrubs immediately after planting settles the soil and eliminates any air pockets. After that, in the absence of adequate rainfall, water thoroughly approximately every 5 days—more often if you live in a hot, dry environment, or less often if you live in a cool, damp climate. After the first 3 or 4 months, begin to taper the frequency of watering. Once the root system is completely established, water your plant on the same schedule as the rest of your garden [see Watering Landscape Trees and Shrubs, pg. 76].

Mulching young trees and shrubs is also important, since among the many benefits of mulching is the soil's increased ability to retain moisture [see Mulches, pg. 82]. For now, place a layer of mulch 3–4 inches (75–100 mm) deep over the entire root zone, being careful to keep the mulch from touching the trunk of the tree.

Protect tree trunks by keeping lawn mowers, string trimmers, and other sharp tools at a safe distance. Remove any plastic tags or wire ties that were attached to the plant when you acquired it in order to keep them from girdling the limbs later.

Avoid walking over the roots, since foot traffic compacts the soil. And if a tree is in an area where children might run into it during play, you can place stakes a short distance from the trunk as a reminder that the tree is out-of-bounds.

If you live in an area with a lot of wildlife, or if you have pets that might be tempted to chew on a newly planted tree, you can protect the tree trunk with a circle of wire mesh [see Autumn Care for Winter Dormancy, pg. 86]. And because young trees are susceptible to the effects of hot sun and winter cold, consider protecting a tree's trunk with strips of burlap or trunk wrap [see Trunk Wrapping, pg. 86].

Finally, it is a good idea to write in a notebook the names of the trees and shrubs you have planted. When questions come up in future years, you will know exactly what each plant is. It's also fun to jot down the date you planted each tree and even to take a photograph of your newly planted trees and shrubs. Later, you'll look back and marvel at how the plants have grown, and you'll be amazed at your garden's transformation.

While established trees generally are drought-resistant, water your new plantings whenever the soil surface has dried to a depth of 6 inches (15 cm) or more unless the care instructions for the species make other recommendation. Waterings should continue for the first two seasons of growth.

FIRST WATERINGS AND FERTILIZING

Watering new tree and shrub plantings helps ease transplant shock, replaces water lost in the soil surrounding the roots, prompts new growth, and settles the soil. Fertilize shrubs by properly preparing soil [see Amending and Fertilizing Soil, pg. 46]. Apply foliar fertilizer—water-soluble nutrients absorbed through foliage, stems, and roots—to give your plants a boost soon after planting. Water and fertilize by following these easy steps:

Watering

1 Slowly apply water to trees and shrubs at the rate it is absorbed, until the ground becomes saturated. This may mean refilling the moated watering basin several times.

2 If a deep-watering system was installed for your tree, fill it to overflowing, allow it to drain, then refill it. Add extra soil to fill any slump or settling.

3 Water every 48 hours for the first 10 days after planting. Irrigate weekly thereafter, allowing the soil's surface to dry between applications, to a depth of 4–6 in. (10–15 cm).

Foliar Fertilizing

1 Most foliar fertilizers are water-soluble powders. Don rubber gloves and mix a solution of fertilizer and water at half the package-recommended rate for your hose-end sprayer.

2 Fill a hose-end sprayer with the diluted solution. Set the applicator as recommended for the sprayer and fertilizer.

3 On a calm, warm morning, spray the foliage, stem or trunk, and branches of the shrub or tree until thoroughly wetted with fertilizer spray. Allow it to dry before evening.

Y our love of the outdoors and of all things that grow will undoubtedly increase as you care for your garden over the years. Each season you will notice something new, and you'll come to a deeper appreciation of the distinctive traits of each plant.

Pruning, watering, and fertilizing are all key issues in the care of plants. Pruning young plants can help direct their growth, while cutting back older plants can promote flowering and fruiting, give plants a more pleasing shape, and keep them healthy and disease-free. In the following pages, you'll learn the basics of when and how to prune deciduous trees and shrubs as well as needle-leaved and broad-leaved evergreens. You'll be taken step-by-step through the processes of rejuvenating an older shrub, pruning to shape a conifer, opening up a mature tree to let in more light, and pollarding—a technique of winter pruning that promotes vigorous new growth in the spring.

Care and Maintenance

Also in this chapter, you'll see how to water newly planted as well as established trees and shrubs, install an automatic irrigation system, fertilize your plants, and apply mulch. And you'll find out about the special care needs of container plants.

Finally, you will explore the topic of pests and diseases in your landscape. Plants that are well adapted to your site and soil, and pruned, watered, and fertilized in the recommended way, will be strong, healthy, and able to resist most pests or diseases. If pests or diseases do become evident, prompt care quickly will return the plants to a robust state. The chart in this chapter will help you identify any irregularities in your garden and guide you in taking the necessary steps to bring your plants back to a healthy state [see Common Tree and Shrub Pest and Disease Solutions, pg. 85].

If you garden in a cold-winter climate, you'll want to use the suggestions on autumn care for winter dormancy, including a tip on how to protect grafted roses and other tender shrubs from winter freezing.

> **Learn how to water and prune your trees and shrubs, plus tips on preparing them for winter**

A hedge planting receives its first pruning. In the growing season just passed, it established its roots and sent up new growth. Now it's time to begin training the young plants into the formal shapes in which they will be maintained throughout their lives.

PRUNING BASICS

The three T's of pruning are timing, tools, and technique. Each is important to successfully managing the growth of trees and shrubs. You'll explore the tools and techniques for pruning in the following pages. For now, let's look at timing first.

Timing is affected primarily by the climate in which the plant is growing, the nature of the plant being pruned, and what you are trying to achieve. Fortunately, there are several guidelines to help you. Generally, the shaping of a young deciduous tree or the removal of a large limb from a mature deciduous tree is best done toward the end of the dormant season, when the trees are still leafless and before growth begins in the spring. Shaping of evergreen trees, however, is most readily accomplished in spring or early summer.

For flowering shrubs, the time of pruning is guided by the time of bloom. Spring-flowering shrubs such as azalea, forsythia, and weigela are normally pruned after they bloom. This allows their flower buds to set naturally in the autumn and provides for a nice flower display the following spring. On the other hand, summer-blooming shrubs are best pruned in the dormant winter season, since their flower buds form on new growth, which begins to develop in the spring. Among the summer-blooming shrubs that benefit from dormant season pruning are abelia, heavenly bamboo, beauty bush, crape myrtle, cranberry bush, viburnum, and sweet shrub.

Shrubs that are grown for their foliage rather than their flowers can be pruned during late winter, spring, or early summer. Pruning typically generates a flush of new growth right below each cut; thus pruning in late winter or early spring is most effective for making a shrub fuller or bushier. Summer pruning is necessary for trimming wayward shoots or cutting away unwanted suckers from a shrub's rootstock.

As a general rule, pruning during the autumn or early winter months should be avoided. Pruning at that time of year may encourage tender new growth that is subject to frost damage by the winter cold. You can cut away diseased or dead wood on a tree or shrub at any time of the year; make this, and regular pinching of growth buds to shape growth, part of your routine garden maintenance.

There are two types of hand pruning shears available, anvil and bypass. For shrub and tree pruning, always choose bypass pruners to make the closest cuts and avoid crushing the wood.

PRUNING TOOLS

The right tools make pruning easier, both on you and on your plants. Depending on the scope of your project, hand pruners, lopping shears, pruning saws, or pole pruners will come in handy. For some tasks, it helps to have power saws or trimmers. All are readily available at nurseries and garden centers.

There are two basic types of hand pruners: bypass and anvil models. Bypass pruners work like scissors, with two sharp blades that glide against each other. They make clean, smooth cuts. Anvil pruners have one sharp blade that presses against a wide, flat blade, crushing the branch that is being cut. Either type is suitable for cutting branches up to ½ inch (12 mm) in diameter.

Lopping shears have handles about 2 feet (60 cm) in length. Longer handles increase your leverage and allow you to cut branches up to 1½ inches (38 mm) in diameter. For larger limbs, you will most likely require a pruning saw. Straight-bladed and bow saws cut on both the push and the pull strokes and make quick work of limbs up to 3 inches (75 mm) in diameter. For larger limbs, consider a power reciprocating saw.

For high branches, a pole pruner is helpful. A pole pruner has a shearing blade and a small saw at the end of a handle that is 5–8 feet (1.5–2.4 m) long, allowing pruning of limbs that otherwise would be difficult to reach. Whenever you work with overhead limbs, be sure to wear eye-protection goggles, gloves, and a safety helmet.

To keep pruning tools in good shape, wipe their blades with a rag after every use. At the end of each season, clean the blades with a solvent such as mineral oil, then apply a few drops of light lubricating oil to the blades and moving parts. Sharpen bypass pruning shears with a moistened whetstone when needed, remembering to hone only the outside edge of the blades so that the inside surfaces will remain flat and glide closely against each another.

Always choose tools that are appropriate to the size of the task. If your yard is a small urban courtyard, your needs will be more modest than for a gardener with a large woodland yard. Hand tools may work as well for a patio, but consider power tools if your site is extensive.

For instance, if you have several hedges in your garden, a power trimmer will be an asset. Many models are available, with several blade choices: long or short, single or double sided, and with single or double—reciprocating—action. Power trimmers are fueled by gasoline, electricity, or rechargeable battery. A reciprocating saw is another tool that is more handy than a chainsaw for most homeowners. Always wear protective gear—safety glasses, gloves, and ear plugs—when operating power tools to protect you from safety and health hazards.

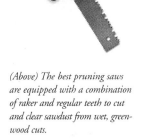

(Above) The best pruning saws are equipped with a combination of raker and regular teeth to cut and clear sawdust from wet, green-wood cuts.

(Left) A pole pruner consists of a pruning saw and shear cutting blade mounted on a telescoping fiberglass or aluminum pole.

(Below) Tree and shrub pruning equipment is available in power and hand models.

PRUNING HEALTHY SHRUBS FOR OPTIMAL GROWTH

There are many reasons to prune shrubs. You may want to control a shrub's size, improve its shape, promote flowering and fruiting, remove dead or diseased stems, create a more open look, or encourage a fuller, leafier appearance. Your goal will influence the type and the timing of your pruning.

It seems paradoxical that pruning a shrub can make it grow back thicker and bushier, but the principles that control a plant's growth make this possible. Every branch has a growing bud at its tip, along with lateral buds lying along its stem. (Run your finger over a bare branch in the winter, and you'll discover this immediately.) The bud at the tip of every branch is the dominant bud, having what is referred to as apical dominance. As long as a branch remains intact,

(Right) Many flowering shrubs bloom on second-year wood, the foliage growth they had during the prior garden season. Pruning in autumn would eliminate the the following year's bloom from such plants; they should be pruned after their blooms fade.

(Below) Pruning a shrub does more than neaten its outline; it controls and directs the shrub's growth while allowing access to structures behind the planting.

the apical bud will grow steadily in a single burst. But if the branch is pruned back and the dominant bud is removed, latent buds below the cut are invigorated to sprout and make a mass of new growth. Thus, lightly pruning all of a shrub's branches will encourage a flush of new growth and make its outer canopy more dense. These types of pruning cuts, which are made at a slight angle just above a lateral bud, are known as heading cuts.

Repeated heading over the years may make some shrubs leggy, as the dense new growth on the plant's outer canopy shades out the shrub's interior. In such a case, thinning cuts can help open up the interior to more sunlight and make the shrub grow thicker throughout. Thinning cuts are similar to heading cuts but are made by reaching deep into the plant's interior and making the cut, or by cutting a branch all the way off at ground level. Such thinning cuts are routinely used in rejuvenation pruning for deciduous shrubs and broad-leaved evergreens and, depending on the plant, are performed in autumn–spring or following bloom [see Rejuvenating an Overgrown Shrub, pg. 68].

SHAPING AND CONTROLLING SHRUB GROWTH

Shaping and training is a continual process, performed throughout the growing season. Shrubs grow at dominant buds found at the ends of their branches. By removing these buds, you force the plant instead to begin new growth at a latent bud. You'll need bypass pruners and gloves, then follow these steps:

1 As the shrub leafs in spring, note the strongest branches and overall shape of the plant. Pinch off leaf buds that later would grow beyond the plant's perimeter.

2 Pinch tender foliage shoots with your finger and thumb, using care to avoid flower buds.

3 After foliage is mature, pinch or cut branch tips to direct growth. If foliage becomes too crowded, remove one-third of the leaves from the area.

4 Strip lateral stems on the main branches. This will allow sunlight to reach the shrub's center and maintain healthy foliage.

5 Prune crossing branches, suckers, and weak joints—branches with narrow angles to the main branch or trunk.

6 Use stiff wire or a rod with plastic stretch tape to bend and train forming branches.

REJUVENATING AN OVERGROWN SHRUB

Sometimes a shrub becomes overgrown and you wish to lower its height or fashion it into a more attractive shape. In this case, rejuvenation, or renovation, pruning is the answer. There are two approaches to rejuvenation pruning: you can cut the overgrown shrub back in one fell swoop or spread the pruning out over several seasons. If you chose the all-at-once approach, cut all the branches back to 6–12 inches (15–30 cm) above ground level at the beginning of the growing season. The shrub will typically

grow a fair amount in the first year after pruning. By the third or fourth year after the pruning, it will be of a fair size and have a lovely, compact shape. From this point on, you can prune it lightly as needed with a combination of heading cuts and thinning cuts to maintain its height and shape.

A more gradual approach to rejuvenation pruning involves cutting one-third of the stems to within 6–12 inches (15–30 cm) of the ground at the beginning of each growing season for 3 years. By the end of this time, all the old wood will be removed and only healthy new growth will remain.

Most deciduous and broad-leaved evergreen shrubs respond well to rejuvenation pruning. However, you should avoid rejuvenation pruning of boxwoods, junipers, and most narrow-leaved evergreens. Instead, when these shrubs become overgrown, consider shaping them into a tree form. This reveals the sculptural qualities of the shrub while giving it a neater look and creating space beneath the shrub for planting ground covers, flowers, or bulbs.

(Right) Individual shrubs have grown together and soon will compete for light. It's time to restore their individuality by pruning them.

(Below) After pruning, each shrub has a distinct outline. All extra branches have been cut, and the perimeter outline of the shrub allows air to circulate to all parts of the plant.

To give a shrub a multistemmed treelike appearance, select three or four of the sturdier limbs to remain as the tree trunk. Keep these limbs intact, while removing all the other low-growing branches. Hawthorns, hollies, serviceberries, and wax myrtles are particularly attractive when pruned this way.

REJUVENATION PRUNING FOR SHRUBS

Woody shrubs that have grown too large, suffered damage, or become leggy or misshapen sometimes require restoration. Prune species that bloom on second-year wood after they bloom, while cutting back other deciduous shrubs in autumn after leaves fall. Prune evergreen shrubs in spring. Gather gloves, hand shears, and lopping shears, then follow these steps:

1 Remove all dead wood, broken branches, or those with sign of disease such as fungus, borers, or dripping sap.

2 Remove branches and laterals that cross the centerline of the shrub. Trim off suckers and any sprouts from the main trunk.

3 Note the basic outline of the shrub, trimming back all branches that extend more than 4 in. (10 cm) past its preferred profile.

4 If foliage at the shrub's center is stunted or yellow, reduce the number of branches to allow light to penetrate to the center, making cuts at trunk or stem.

5 Finally, reduce the number of branch laterals to further open the shrub's interior to light through the canopy.

PRUNING EVERGREEN TREES

Evergreen trees typically require little pruning. However, conifers may benefit from shaping to enhance their natural look, or from light pruning to promote density.

For pruning purposes, conifers can be divided into three groups—pines, conifers such as spruce and fir whose branches whorl off a main trunk like spokes from an axis, and those such as arborvitae and junipers that have soft growth and random, unwhorled branches.

On pines, you can encourage dense foliage by pruning back the growing tips before the needles unfold. To do this, wait until the spring or early summer when the immature needles are packed around the stem and resemble candles. When the developing candles have reached their full length and while the needles are still soft, cut the candles back to one-half of their length.

Broad-leaved evergreen trees such as olive should be pruned in spring after their growth slows. Follow the same approach as you would use for a deciduous tree, removing dead and crossing branches, preserving the strongest leaders, and limiting growth to the tree outline.

CREATING A TOPIARY

Creating an evergreen topiary is an excellent way to express your personal style in your garden—whether your style is formal and classical or whimsical and fun-loving [see Hedges, Topiary, and Espalier, pg. 9]. Although many kinds of plants can be used to create topiaries, boxwood, holly, and yew are particularly good choices.

To fashion a topiary from a young plant, place a wire frame of the shape you desire over the plant. As the plant begins to grow through the frame, trim it back to within 2–3 inches (50–75 mm) of the frame, using the frame as a guide. Continue to cut the plant back as necessary from spring through late summer, refraining from any pruning during the autumn or winter months.

Firs, spruces, and related evergreens have a naturally symmetrical growth habit that is very attractive, and they rarely need anything more than shaping. Lightly prune them in winter and use their branches for your holiday decorations. When pruning, always make your cuts so that living, green tissue is left on a stem [see Shape Pruning a Conifer, next pg.].

Arborvitae, hemlocks, junipers, yews, and other conifers with a random branching habit can take heavier pruning than other conifers. They may be pruned any time from early spring through the middle of summer, although they will grow back most quickly after pruning in the spring. It is always best to avoid cutting into hardened older wood. Instead, be sure some green foliage remains on the part of the branches you cut back.

Evergreens—especially pines and yew—are sometimes pruned to create sculptural interest in a garden. By cutting off selected branches, you can reveal the interesting bends and forms in some of the other branches, leaving needle groups isolated at their tips and along their lengths. This sculpted look has long been part of Japanese-themed gardens and can be used to bring an oriental note to your landscape.

SHAPE PRUNING A CONIFER

1 If conifers develop a forked top, cut away one of the leading shoots with hand shears. The remaining leader will divide and fill the top with new branches.

Young, needle-bearing evergreen trees can be lightly pruned and shaped to restore symmetry and balance due to irregular growth. Such pruning is best done in spring, when the tree is actively growing distinctive new foliage, or so-called candles of new needles. Gather hand pruners, a pruning saw, and gloves, then follow these steps:

2 Remove entire branches by making a first cut, upward and halfway into the underside of the branch, 4–6 in. (10–15 cm) from the trunk.

3 Remove the branch by cutting downward from the top, ½ in. (12 mm) outside the first cut. These cuts avoid skinning bark from the tree.

4 Finally, neaten the cut and prevent disease by cutting off the stub at the shoulder.

5 For conifers—cedar, fir, pine, spruce— make shaping cuts, 2–4 in. (50–100 mm) long, into the new candles with hand shears. Avoid cuts into old needle areas; they would kill the branch.

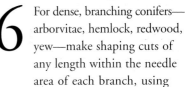

6 For dense, branching conifers— arborvitae, hemlock, redwood, yew—make shaping cuts of any length within the needle area of each branch, using hand shears.

PRUNING DECIDUOUS TREES

Pruning of deciduous trees can be used to shape a young tree, to keep a mature tree healthy, or to allow more light into a mature tree's canopy.

When working with a young tree, the goal is to provide it with a good framework for future growth. For a shade tree, the ideal structure is a strong central trunk with five to eight branches radiating from the trunk at different heights. At the beginning of each growing season, remove branches that grow inward or rub across nearby limbs, as well as any branches that are growing at angles of less than 45 degrees to the main trunk. As the young trees grow, gradually remove lower branches to raise the crown to the desired height.

Before trimming, examine the tree to identify the branch collar—the ring of rough bark that encircles the area where a limb attaches to the trunk. When pruning, cut just outside the branch collar. Leave the cut open to the air—avoid wound-dressing compounds, which once were commonly used but are now considered unnecessary.

(Right) Training a container tree into an espalier is easy. Here, a Benjamin tree, a type of fig, was planted into a spacious container and a lattice frame was inserted into the rootball's side. Some of the branches were selected for tying, others for removal. In time, the tree will assume the typical, flat shape characteristic of espalier.

(Below) Use a battery-powered reciprocating saw to neaten dead branches and remove limbs that cross back through the center of the tree, keeping it open.

On mature trees, you should prune out decaying branches, since they can threaten the overall health of the tree. Also remove any crossed limbs—this helps the remaining branches stay strong and has the added advantage of letting dappled sunlight into the shrub layer below.

If you are removing a large limb from a mature tree, use the three-cut method. Make the first cut on the underside of the limb, about 1-foot (30 cm) from the main trunk. This cut, which should extend about one-quarter of the way through the limb, will keep the bark from tearing. Make the second cut from the top, about 1 inch (25 mm) beyond the bottom cut. Cut all the way through the limb, leaving a 1 inch (25-mm) stub. With your third cut you will remove the stub flush with the tree's branch collar.

Make a habit of checking your trees every year. If heavy pruning is required on large trees, consult with an expert such as a certified arborist or a tree surgeon.

ANNUAL PRUNING AND IN-SEASON MAINTENANCE OF DECIDUOUS TREES

Pruning deciduous trees channels growth to their strongest branches. Prune flowering species after they bloom if they form flowers on their second-year wood; otherwise, prune in autumn after leaves fall. Gather hand shears, a pole pruner, lopping shears, a pruning saw, and gloves, then follow these steps:

1 Remove all dead wood, broken branches, or those with sign of disease such as fungus, borers, or dripping sap.

2 Remove branches and laterals that cross the centerline of the tree. Trim off suckers and sprouts from the main trunk.

3 Make the tree more compact by pruning terminal branches at their end, or at each end of forking branches.

4 On rounded species, remove vertical shoots growing from the crown's top to create a smooth, dense, rounded head.

5 On conical or upright species, cut away shoots and branches that break the tree's outer plane to restore symmetry.

6 Some trees and shrubs produce suckers at their root crown. Prune them away to maintain a treelike appearance.

POLLARDING DECIDUOUS TREES

Pollarding is a popular pruning method used to encourage abundant annual foliage in a ball-like habit. It is best used for fast-growing trees such as fruitless mulberry and willow in a formal setting. Prune the tree in autumn for greatest seasonal growth or in spring before leaf buds form to retard growth. Gather a sturdy tree ladder, chalk, tape measure, pole pruner, pruning saw, and gloves, then follow these steps:

1 Three to six main branches should extend equally from the tree's center. Mark main cuts with chalk at a point with nascent buds.

2 Remove all lateral shoots on each primary branch with abundant growth buds, from the marks to the trunk.

3 At the marks, cut off the branches with a pruning saw, cutting upward from the underside of the branch. Make a second, downward cut to remove the limb without skinning the branch.

4 Remove all of the secondary branches from the tree with a long-handled pruner, cutting them flush with the trunk.

5 In the second and subsequent seasons, use pole pruners or a pruning saw to remove each long new-growth sprout at its junction with the main branch.

REDUCTION PRUNING OF DECIDUOUS TREES

1 Remove any dead, weak, or crossing branches, trimming them flush with the trunk.

Sometimes, owing to care or growing conditions, a deciduous tree requires pruning to restore balance to its shape or to reduce its size. In cases where severe pruning is needed, spread the pruning over two seasons. Reduction prune in autumn after all leaves have fallen, and water faithfully the following season. Gather long-handled pruners, plastic tape, a pole pruner, pruning saw, tree ladder, gloves, and eye-protective goggles, then follow these steps:

2 Evaluate the cuts you'll make by marking them with plastic tape. They should reduce the canopy size by 25–33 percent and be symmetrical.

3 With a pole pruner, remove all small foliage branches outside of the main cut markers, leaving bare branches.

4 Use a pruning saw to remove branches with three cuts: the first halfway and underneath, followed by a second halfway from above and outside the first cut. Finally, cut the stub off at the crotch with the trunk.

5 Select 3–5 laterals from each main branch for retention, then remove the remainder.

6 Spray the pruned tree with horticultural oil to eliminate boring pests and stave off fungal infections.

WATERING LANDSCAPE TREES AND SHRUBS

(Right) Applying mulch and using a slow-application soaker hose to water new tree plantings on hillsides prevents runoff.

(Inset) A water-dispersing hose-end fitting slows the flow and prevents erosion.

(Bottom) Always plant trees and shrubs upright on sloped sites, terracing the planting hole and protecting it with a barrier wall from soil sliding onto the trunk.

How often—and how much—a tree or shrub should be watered is a key question. In the first year or two after being planted, a tree or shrub will benefit from frequent watering. A steady supply of moisture will help the plant establish a strong root system, with healthy roots reaching out and down through the soil. After becoming established, the plant can go for increasingly longer periods without supplemental watering, as its own roots gather moisture from the surrounding soil. Once most trees and shrubs have been in the ground for 2–3 years, they can withstand occasional periods of drought without damage.

The amount of water that newly planted trees or shrubs require depends on the plants and the type of soil in which each is growing. Soils have varying water-storage capacities, with clay soils typically requiring less irrigation than sandy soils. Generally, trees and shrubs require the equivalent of 1 inch (25 mm) of water per week during their first growing season.

Once they have settled in, most trees and shrubs do best with infrequent, deep watering that soaks the soil at least 1 foot (30 cm) deep. Avoid frequent, shallow waterings, since such irrigation encourages root growth near the surface, making the plants more vulnerable during periods of drought and in some cases causing nearby patios or walkways

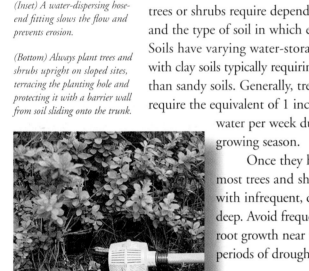

to crack. Watering at the correct time of day also helps keep plants healthy. The guiding principle is to minimize the length of time that the leaves stay wet, since wet foliage often is an invitation to disease. Watering in the morning before 10 a.m. is best.

You can easily determine when to water. With a shovel or soil-sampling tube, dig down into the soil about 8 inches (20 cm). If the soil at that depth is dry, then it's time to water. If you find the soil is moist near the surface but dry below, that's a sign that you need to irrigate more deeply. One way to ensure that water will make its way to a tree's roots is to install deep-watering tubes [see Installing an Automatic Deep-Watering System, next pg.].

Get your newly planted trees and shrubs off to a good start by watering them regularly whenever natural precipitation falls short or drought conditions occur.

INSTALLING AN AUTOMATIC DEEP-WATERING SYSTEM

Deep watering conserves irrigation water, prompts trees to develop deep roots, helps prevent fungal spores from splashing from the soil onto foliage, and avoids runoff and erosion. Install deep-watering tubes when you dig your planting hole [see Digging a Tree-Planting Hole, pg. 51]. Automate your watering by installing a battery-powered irrigation-control valve and plastic drip line with emitters at the tube, following these steps:

1 Install a threaded Y fitting at the faucet of your hose bib. This allows you to connect a hose or fill a watering can without having to disconnect your drip irrigation system.

2 Read carefully all installation instructions and attach the battery-powered irrigation-control valve to one hose-thread connector on the Y fitting. Thread adapters may be needed for installation.

3 Attach a ½-in. (12-mm) drip irrigation supply line to the control valve, using a hose clamp or threaded fitting. Run the line to each tree's deep-watering tube.

4 Use a power drill fitted with a ¼-in. (6-mm) bit to bore a hole in the side of the deep-watering tube.

5 Install a lateral line with shrub bubbler emitter at the tube. Seal the deep-watering tube with a removable PVC cap to prevent debris and pests from entering the tube.

6 Turn on the water to the control valve at the Y fitting. Set the timer for weekly operation and a duration to deliver 3–5 gal. (11–19 l) of water at each application.

CARING FOR CONTAINER TREES AND SHRUBS

Key steps in the care of container plants: mounting the pot on a raised, rolling platform; applying fertilizer; staking; care during frost; and moving the plant inside during prolonged times of cold or in winter.

Trees and shrubs that are planted in containers have special maintenance needs. They typically require more frequent watering and feeding than do those planted in the open ground, since potting soil usually dries out quickly.

The amount and frequency of watering required depends on many factors, including the size of the container in relation to the tree or shrub it contains, the amount of sun the plant receives, and the porosity of the container. The goal is to keep the soil moist during the growing season, without letting it stay overly soggy. The best way to determine when to water is to press your finger 2–3 inches (50–75 mm) into the soil. If the soil is dry at that depth, treat your plant to a good soaking. For ease, install drip irrigation [see Installing Drip Irrigation Systems for Containers, next pg.]. You'll probably notice that during the dormant season, when it's normally rainy, you'll need to water less often, if at all.

One side effect of the frequent irrigation of container plants is that nutrients, which reside as salts and minerals in the growing medium, are leached—dissolved into the water—and carried away. To keep your containerized tree or shrub healthy, you will need to supplement the potting medium with fertilizer on a regular basis, either by applying a water-soluble fertilizer or by sprinkling granular fertilizers over the top of the container soil [see Applying Fertilizers to Trees and Shrubs, pg. 81]. Regardless of which type of fertilizer you use, it is important to read carefully and follow exactly all package directions regarding timing and amount.

In addition to regular watering and fertilizing, there are some other maintenance tasks you should perform from time to time. If your plant is stagnating, or if you are having to water on a daily basis even when temperatures are moderate, you most likely need to repot the plant, placing it in a larger container. If so, it is best to use a pot with a diameter of 4–6 inches (10–15 cm) wider than its current container. When repotting, fan out the root system, unwinding any roots that were growing in circles around the interior of the old pot. Water the plant thoroughly after repotting, and then apply a finishing layer of mulch over the top of the soil.

It's a good practice to gently remove the top inch (25 mm) of soil from the container every other year and replace it with fresh potting mix.

Every 4–5 years, remove the tree or shrub from its container for remedial root pruning. Cut back the tips of all the visible roots and prune out most of the larger, woody roots before repotting. Generally, you can return the plant to the same container. Finally, strip leaves equivalent in area to the quantity of roots removed to help the plant adjust, begin new growth, and quickly recover. You should begin to see new foliage sprouting in 3–4 weeks. Following this procedure will keep your plant's root system healthy and viable for many years, prolonging the life of your tree or shrub.

INSTALLING DRIP IRRIGATION SYSTEMS FOR CONTAINERS

Drip irrigation is an efficient and practical means to provide water to your shrub and tree plantings. Most garden centers and hardware retailers have all of the components needed for a home drip system. Because containers have limited space, they are ideal applications for drip irrigation. Drip systems either may be added to existing in-ground irrigation fixtures or set up as individual circuits, following these steps:

A If you have an in-ground irrigation system, replace an existing spray head to meet your plant's needs. Install a drip irrigation fitting, then follow the simple directions below.

B For a new drip system, attach a Y fitting at the faucet of your hose bib. Attach a battery-powered irrigation-control valve to one of the connectors on the Y fitting. Attach a drip-irrigation fitting, then follow the simple directions below.

1 Attach ½-in. (12-mm) drip irrigation supply line to the control valve with a hose clamp or threaded fitting. Run the line to each plant container.

2 Use a piercing tool to punch a hole in the supply line, then fit a lateral connector into the line and attach a drip emitter. Choose emitters with flow rates appropriate to your plant's needs.

3 Place the emitter low in the pot, avoiding sites where it will spray foliage. Use an emitter stake to hold it in place.

4 Turn the system on and make any final adjustments to the emitter locations. Then set the timer for the interval and duration that's appropriate to your container plants' needs.

FERTILIZING TREES AND SHRUBS

Trees growing in soils to which they are naturally adapted—whether it be the rich loam of a forest or the sandy terrain of a beachfront—typically thrive on their own, without the addition of fertilizers. Of course, the conditions in our yards rarely mimic a tree's optimal environment, so in some cases it is necessary to help a tree along by providing additional nutrients.

(Right) Choose fertilizers by their nutritional analysis and acid content. Apply fertilizers at the recommended time and interval for the species.

(Below) Consider adding a hose-end fertilizer applicator to your tools, especially for use with plants in containers or those planted in beds with loose soil.

The only time you need to fertilize a tree is when you must correct a nutritional deficit.

You can spot most deficiencies by unusual coloration in a tree's leaves. Yellow leaves on a tree that normally bears green foliage is often a sign of either a nitrogen or iron deficiency. With a nitrogen shortage, the entire leaf turns yellow and may drop off, while with an iron deficiency the veins of the leaf remain green even as the rest of the leaf turns yellow. Leaves may be smaller compared to those of other trees of the same species growing in your garden. Also, new twig growth may be shorter than in past years.

If you notice any of these symptoms, first rule out any disease or pests as the cause [see Pests and Diseases, pg. 84]. Should you suspect a nutritional deficiency, perform a soil test [see Testing Soil, pg. 33]. When the test indicates a shortage, follow its recommendations regarding the amount and type of fertilizer to use. Generally, flower and fruit trees need additional potassium and phosphorus, while most others require nitrogen. An iron deficiency is usually treated with chelated iron. On loose sandy soils broadcast the fertilizer over an area twice the diameter of the tree's canopy. If your soil is clayey or compacted, you can bore holes in the soil around the tree's drip line—the area beneath the outer edge of the tree's canopy—and fill the holes with a slow-release fertilizer, which will feed the roots at a prescribed rate over a period of time.

Shrubs, especially flowering species, may need to be fed more often than trees. Use a light application of all-purpose fertilizer in the spring and again in the summer. Feed more frequently if there is a nutritional deficiency, as indicated by unusual leaf coloration and confirmed by a soil test. Whenever you apply fertilizers, it's a good idea to keep in mind a simple message: when in doubt, less is better than more. You can always add additional fertilizer at a later date, but it is difficult to undo the damage done by too heavy an application of fast-acting chemicals. Also be sure to water well after any application of fertilizer to avoid burning your plants.

APPLYING FERTILIZERS TO TREES AND SHRUBS

A Apply liquid and water-soluble fertilizers to the soil around the plant's drip line, an imaginary circle on the ground under the outermost foliage.

F ertilizers are available in natural, organic, inorganic, synthetic, liquid, dry, and water-soluble forms. The composition analysis is on the package, a trio of numbers such as 10–10–10 that tells the relative percentage by weight of nitrogen, phosphorus, and potassium in the fertilizer. Nitrogen fuels foliage development, while phosphorus and potassium help nutrient transport between roots, stems, and leaves and promote general vigor. For most tree and shrub applications, a complete, balanced fertilizer is best. To apply various fertilizers, choose from these options.

B Apply dry, granular, and synthetic fertilizers by sprinkling them onto the soil around the plant, then working them into the soil with a hand fork or claw. Water after application.

C Apply natural manure and inorganic mineral fertilizers by spreading them across the soil surface around the plant. Work them into the surface with a rake, fork, or claw. Water after application.

D Apply organic compost to the soil in a layer, 2–3 in. (50–75 mm) thick, avoiding contact with shrub stems or tree trunks. Water after application.

E Apply foliar fertilizers using a hose-end sprayer set to the package-recommended application rate. Choose a time early on a calm, warm day to allow foliage to dry before evening.

MULCHES

Mulch is a material—such as pine, straw, wood or bark chips, or salt hay—that is spread on the ground around the base of plants. In addition to making your garden more attractive by providing a sense of neatness and giving your beds definition, mulches perform a number of vital functions in a garden. Because of their insulating effects, they create a favorable environment for plant roots: they keep soils warmer in the winter and cooler in the summer, and in cold climates they help prevent damage by reducing the number of freeze-thaw cycles. Mulches conserve water by reducing surface evaporation, and they improve soil texture and nutrient value as they decompose. By lowering the incidence of soil-borne diseases and keeping weed growth down, mulches keep plants healthy while reducing yard maintenance.

As mulch is slowly broken down by natural biological processes, it affects your soil's pH by releasing either slightly acidic or slightly alkaline substances. As a general rule, pine straw, pine bark, cypress, and eucalyptus products release acid, while hardwood mulches release alkaline substances. You can use this fact to your advantage by putting acid-releasing mulches around acid-loving plants such as rhododendrons, and hardwood mulches around plants that like neutral or alkaline conditions.

To be effective, a layer of mulch should be 2–3 inches (50–75 mm) deep. Make sure the soil is moist, then apply the mulch throughout a planting bed or, if you wish, to the root zone of a single plant. Always leave a space of 3–4 inches (75–100 mm) between any tree trunks and the mulch. This mulch-free zone will help prevent basal rot from developing on the trunks.

Applying mulch to the soil around your shrubs and trees mimics the conditions found in woodlands and forests. It preserves moisture, limits soil erosion, and moderates changes in temperature to limit frost heaving in areas with cold-winter climates and overheating in those with arid climates.

When the mulch layer has decomposed to the point that there is only 1 inch (25 mm) left, replenish it by applying new mulch after raking and removing the old layer. How often you will need to do this depends on your climate and on the type of mulch you are using; typically, bark chips outlast pine needles and straw. You'll probably need to replenish mulch only about once a year.

APPLYING MULCH IN THE LANDSCAPE

Mulch performs several useful functions in the landscape in addition to dressing up your beds and borders. It helps conserve water, blocks sunlight from weed seeds to prevent their germination, and, if organic, decomposes slowly to release nutrients that fertilize your trees and shrubs. Mulches include bark and wood chips, compost, salt grass hay, decomposed granite, and cocoa hulls, among others. Gather mulch, a garden cart, a fine-tined mulch rake, and gloves, then follow these steps:

1 Rake, remove, and discard any old mulch that remains before adding new mulch. This step also removes leaf litter, insect eggs, fungal spores, and soil disease organisms.

2 Use a garden cart to place piles of mulch spaced throughout the area.

3 Rake the mulch into an even layer, 2–3 in. (50–75 mm) thick. Keep the mulch 3–4 in. (75–100 mm) away from your shrub stems and tree trunks.

PESTS AND DISEASES

When it comes to keeping your trees and shrubs healthy, an ounce of prevention is worth a pound of cure. Well-maintained, healthy plants are less susceptible to pests than stressed or injured plants, and they are better equipped to shrug off disease. To keep your plants healthy, water each plant according to its needs, avoiding either overwatering or underwatering. Make sure that there is good air circulation between and within plants, since this will protect against fungal or bacterial outbreaks. Also, always keep your garden neat by removing weeds and debris—weeds weaken other plants by competing for water and nutrients, and debris shelters undesirable pests. Make sure the soil's pH is adjusted to suit the plant species being grown, and fertilize only as indicated by a soil test.

(Right) Protect a tender plant from animal pests by building a fence around it that extends both above and below the ground.

(Above) Beetles of various types will damage tender shoots and flower buds. Hand picking and application of insecticidal soap directly to the pest are effective means of control.

(Below) When choosing garden pesticides and fungicides, identify the specific pest or disease that is causing the condition, match it to the listing on the label, and check that the agent is approved for use on your plant. Always read completely and follow exactly all the package-label instructions when using garden chemicals.

One of the best things you can do for your plants' health is to get into the habit of frequently walking through your garden. Look carefully at each plant, keeping an eye out for discolored or tattered foliage or anything else that seems amiss. Should you notice any signs of disease or pests, refer to the chart on the opposite page. Since proper identification is important, you can take a typical leaf to your USDA, Agriculture Canada, or university extension agent, or to a nursery or garden center, where the staff can provide a diagnosis.

If you find pests in your garden, study all your options before taking action. About 90–95 percent of all insects found in home landscapes are either beneficial or harmless. Most plants can tolerate quite a bit of foliage loss or other damage without serious consequence. The environmentally safe practices of hand picking any visible pests, knocking pests off a plant with a strong stream of water from a garden hose, or pruning out any diseased portions of the affected plant may be the only steps you'll need to take. To avoid spreading disease, sterilize your shears between cuts by dipping them in dilute bleach solution.

For resistant conditions, you may have to use spot applications of stronger controls such as horticultural oils or insecticidal soap solutions, available at nurseries and garden centers. Any control you use in your garden should list on the label the specific disease or pest you're treating, and should be carefully applied in accordance with the manufacturer's printed instructions.

COMMON TREE AND SHRUB PEST AND DISEASE SOLUTIONS

Symptom	Cause	Remedies
Silvery spots on upper surfaces of leaves; black spots on undersides of leaves.	Lace bugs. Bugs are 1/8–1/4 inch (3–6 mm) in length. Common during the growing season on rhododendrons, laurels, hawthorns, and elms.	Wash off light infestations with a strong stream of water. If necessary, spray with superior oil. Spray with botanical neem or pyrethrin as a last resort.
Leaves curled and twisted, often with a black sooty appearance. Stunted or deformed blooms on new growth.	Aphids. Soft-bodied insects, 1/4-inch (6-mm) long, varying in color from green to yellow to black. Common on a wide range of plants.	Wash off light infestations with a strong stream of water. If ineffective, spray with superior oil. Spray with botanical neem or pyrethrin as a last resort.
Weakened and defoliated trees and shrubs. Small, silken bags about 1–2 in. (25–50 mm) long hanging from branches.	Bagworms. Caterpillars hidden by silky bag. In North America, east of the Rocky Mountains. Found on deciduous plants and conifers; worst damage on arborvitae and cedars.	For small infestations, hand pick and destroy bags. For large infestations, spray with *Bacillus thuringiensis* (Bt) as soon as young bagworms are noticed.
Green parts of leaves are removed and veins remain. Later, leaves are dry and skeletonized.	Beetles, including Japanese beetles, elm leaf beetles, and willow leaf beetles. Hard-shelled beetles are most active in the heat of the day.	Hand pick beetles on small shrubs in early morning while they are inactive. Apply milky spore (*Bacillus popilliae*) to lawns to give long-term control for Japanese beetle grubs.
In spring and summer, silky webs, or tents, appear in the forks of small limbs, and leaves are eaten. In winter, masses of eggs encircle stems.	Tent caterpillars. Adult caterpillars are 1–2 in. (25–50 mm) long with short fuzzy bodies. Common only on deciduous trees and shrubs.	In winter, remove egg masses from bare branches. In spring, prune branches with small tents and destroy clippings. If necessary, spray with insecticidal soap or *Bacillus thuringiensis* (Bt).
In summer and autumn, silky webs appear at the tip end of branches, with larvae visible inside. Leaves are chewed.	Fall webworms. Adult webworms are about 1 in. (25 mm) long with a dark stripe down their backs. Common on deciduous trees and shrubs.	Prune and destroy branches infected with webs. If necessary, spray with *Bacillus thuringiensis* (Bt) after breaking open web with a stick.
Leaves are bronzed or yellowed, curled, and dried; may fall off. Plants stunted. Webs may be present.	Spider mites and other mites. Microscopic size and therefore difficult to see. Prevalent in hot, dry areas on both conifers and deciduous plants.	Wash off light infestations with a strong stream of water. If necessary, spray with insecticidal soap. Spray with a miticide as a last resort.
Black, tan, or red spots on leaves, and premature leaf drop. Black cankers on stems, with a general wilt of branch tips.	Anthracnose. A fungal disease sometimes called black spot or twig blight. Occurs in late spring and summer, typically after humid conditions.	Remove infected leaves and branch tips. Collect and destroy infected fallen leaves. Thin excessive growth to promote air circulation. Spray with a fungicide as a last resort.
Leaves have white to grayish powdery patches, as though they have been dusted with flour.	Powdery mildew. A fungal disease prevalent when days are hot and nights are cool. Mostly attacks new leaves.	Thin branches to improve air circulation. Spray with a 0.5% solution of baking soda (sodium bicarbonate): 1 tsp. (5 ml) baking soda per quart [1 l] of water.
Young twigs and branches die back, starting at tip ends. Leaves shrivel and turn brown. Tips of twigs curl to resemble a hook.	Fireblight. A bacterial disease common on ornamental pears, crabapples, and quinces. Infection occurs in early spring and is favored by wet conditions.	Prune out branches 6 in. (15 cm) below signs of damage. Dip pruning tool in isopropyl alcohol after each cut to sterilize and prevent spreading infection. Avoid heavy nitrogen fertilization.
Leaves turn light green and are puffy, swollen, and distorted.	Leaf gall. A fungal disease found on azaleas, camellias, and rhododendrons.	Pick off and destroy affected leaves as soon as galls are noticed.
Flowers collapse under heavy fuzz of gray or brown fungal spores.	Botrytis rot, also known as gray mold.	Remove affected blossoms, foliage, or entire plant; space plants for more air circulation; reduce nitrogen fertilizer.

AUTUMN CARE FOR WINTER DORMANCY

If you live in a cold-weather climate, paying a little extra attention to your trees and shrubs in the autumn months can give them the protection they will need to survive the winter without damage.

If autumn rains in your region have been sparse, give plants a deep soaking as the temperatures begin to drop but before the ground freezes. Evergreens particularly will benefit from this treatment, since their leaves continue to release some moisture even in the winter, making them especially susceptible to drying winds.

Newly planted trees and shrubs are less able to withstand cold temperatures than are mature trees and shrubs that have been in the ground for several seasons. However, you can protect young trees and shrubs, as well as trees

While beautiful, winter snows and ice can cause harm to your landscape trees and shrubs. Water is heavy, and the load of snow or ice on branches can cause them to break. Carefully clear such loads from the branches of your trees to avoid hazard to your plants, while wearing a safety helmet and eye-protection glasses for safety.

TRUNK WRAPPING

Newly planted trees whose trunks have yet to develop a thick, corky bark may benefit from trunk wrapping. Trunk wrapping reflects sunlight and reduces the buildup of heat during the day, thus minimizing the temperature fluctuations that cause bark splitting. When you wrap a trunk, use burlap strips or commercial tree wrap. Start at the base of the trunk and wrap toward the top; overlap each strip by ¼–½ in. (6–12 mm). Wrap it up to just below the tree's lower branches, then snugly secure the wrap with twine. Wrap the tree in the autumn and leave the wrapping in place until early spring.

and shrubs that are marginally hardy in your area, by using windbreaks. To construct a windbreak, build a frame of wood stakes or PVC piping around the plant, and then wrap the frame with burlap, canvas, or a similar material. Avoid using non-porous plastics, and make sure to keep the wrapping from touching evergreens to prevent problems caused by condensation. Unwrap the plants in spring after all the likelihood of frost is past.

In some regions, rodents such as mice, porcupine, rabbits, and voles cause tree loss by gnawing the bark off the base of the tree during winter months. If this is a likelihood in your area, you may want to place a guard around the tree. Cut galvanized screen with ¼-inch (6-mm) mesh (sometimes called hardware cloth) into strips 18 inches (45 cm) long, then place the strips around the trunk, with edges overlapping and the lower portion pushed firmly into the ground. This type of guard will last indefinitely and can be left in place all year.

PREPARING SHRUBS FOR WINTER

Cold-winter climates challenge deciduous shrubs and roses that struggle to survive very low temperatures and freezing, especially grafted varieties. Wrapping and seasonal burial of the trunk and branches of plants in autumn protects them with an insulating cover of chips and soil. You'll need a shovel, wood chips, plastic sheeting, and wooden stakes. Follow these steps:

Wrapping Shrubs and Roses

1 Allow roses to develop hips by leaving last blooms on the rose. Avoid pruning them after their last bloom.

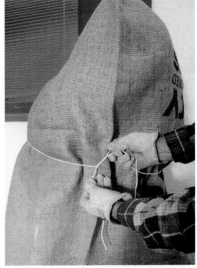

2 Mulch shrubs heavily with straw or cypress mulch, wrap in burlap, then securely tie the covering in place.

3 Cover the wrapped plant with 8–10 in. (20–25 cm) of mulch, then bury it in loose garden soil at least 6 in. (15 cm) deep.

Minnesota Tip for Roses

1 Gently free half the rootball at the base of the rose, taking care to avoid damaging major roots.

2 Apply wood chips to soil to make a bed. Tip the rose toward its still-rooted side, laying it flat on the ground. Stake or peg it into place.

3 Layer over the rose with wood chips 12–18 in. (30–45 cm) thick, cover the chips with burlap, add 12 in. (30 cm) more straw, then cover the mound with loose soil.

Choosing trees and shrubs for your landscape begins as you match your needs to the requirements of each plant

Those who plant trees and shrubs in containers or their landscape usually choose their plants to match a needed appearance trait. Fitting a tree to your needs requires thought and effort, since there are thousands of available cultivars. In setting out to choose the plants in this section, care was taken to profile those trees and shrubs that are among the most successful and popular varieties.

The 48 shrubs and small trees and the 78 landscape trees featured on the following pages include deciduous and evergreen, conifer and broad-leaved, flowering and foliage plants.

This colorful encyclopedia is a visual identification guide as well as your source of accurate and timely information about the most widely planted trees and shrubs for home landscapes. When you admire trees that you see in a private or public garden near your home, compare them to the photographs found here and use the information provided to decide how they can beautify your land-

Encyclopedia of Landscape Trees & Shrubs

scape. Each plant is listed first by its common name, followed by any regional common name variations, then by scientific name and its family. Both the common and scientific names are found in the book's index. Common names vary by areas and regions—when you acquire a plant, check its scientific name to be sure it really is the one you want. There's a wealth of other information given for each plant, including its habit, foliage, flower, and fruit; its bloom season; plant hardiness; complete planting, spacing, and care instructions; plus features that make it distinctive and desirable and information about pest and disease resistance.

Use this encyclopedia as a guide to finding the trees and shrubs that will succeed in your landscape. Check for plants well adapted to the conditions—the soil, sun, wind, and other climate factors—in your yard and plant hardiness zone [see USDA Plant Hardiness Around the World, pg. 132]. Note any special needs they may have for soil, light, watering, fertilizing, pruning, mulching, propagation, or post-bloom care.

(Clockwise from top left) Your enjoyment of trees and shrubs begins when you select those you will plant in your yard. Start your search by discovering these striking landscape plants: California pepper tree, common oleander, callery pear 'Chanticleer', and mountain pine.

SHRUBS AND SMALL TREES

Shrub: Abelia, Glossy. *Abelia × grandiflora.* CAPRIFOLIACEAE.
Description: Several hybrids of medium-growth, dense, semi-evergreen shrubs, 6–8 ft. (1.8–2.5 m) tall and wide, with shiny, bronze to light green or variegated, oval, pointed leaves, turning purple, red in autumn.
Blooms/Berries: Many small, fluted, trumpetlike, pink or white flowers, to ¾ in. (19 mm) long, in summer–early autumn, forming upright or dangling clusters, with dry berrylike, seeded fruit in autumn.
Plant hardiness: Zones 5–9. Ground hardy zones 6–9.
Soil: Moist, well-drained humus. Fertility: Rich–average. 5.5–6.5 pH.
Planting: Full sun. Space 4–6 ft. (1.2–1.8 m) apart.
Care: Easy. Allow surface soil to dry between waterings until established. Fertilize quarterly spring–autumn. Prune sparingly in autumn. Protect from wind. Propagate by cuttings.
Features: Good choice for accents, backgrounds, hedges in formal, woodland gardens. Dwarf hybrids available. Humidity tolerant. Pest, disease resistant.

Shrub: Arborvitae, American. *Thuja occidentalis.* ARBORVITAE.
Description: Over 50 cultivars of slow-growing, mounding or narrow, coniferous, evergreen small trees, to 60 ft. (18 m) tall, with cedarlike, dark green needles with lighter undersides, in upright fans, turning russet, yellow in winter.
Blooms/Cones: Tiny flowers in spring form ½-in. (12-mm) cones in summer.
Plant hardiness: Zones 3–8.
Soil: Moist, well-drained. Fertility: Rich. 6.5–8.0 pH.
Planting: Full sun. Space 4–10 ft. (1.2–3.0 m) apart, depending on use.
Care: Easy. Keep soil moist. Fertilize quarterly spring–autumn. Train to desired shape while young. Protect from drying wind, zones 3–5. Propagate by cuttings, grafting, seed.
Features: Good choice for accents, containers, fences, hedges, screens in woodland gardens and landscapes. Best in cool, humid climates. Deer and spider mite susceptible.

Shrub: Arrowwood. *Viburnum* species. CAPRIFOLIACEAE.
Description: About 225 species of medium-growth, open, deciduous or evergreen shrubs, 5–40 ft. (1.5–12.2 m) tall depending on species, with textured, yellow green, oval, toothed leaves, 3–8 in. (75–200 mm) long, turning red in autumn.
Blooms/Berries: Abundant, sometimes fragrant, white, five-petaled flowers in late spring, 3–5 in. (75–125 mm) wide, forming showy, ball-like clusters, with bright red or black berries in autumn.
Plant hardiness: Zones 3–8, depending on species.
Soil: Moist, well-drained. Fertility: Rich. 6.0–7.5 pH.
Planting: Full sun–partial shade. Space 4–10 ft. (1.2–3.0 m) apart, depending on species and use.
Care: Easy. Keep soil moist. Fertilize annually in spring. Mulch, zones 6–8. Prune sparingly after bloom. Propagate by cuttings, layering, seed.
Features: Good choice for accents, borders, edgings, paths in cottage, natural, wildlife, woodland gardens and landscapes. Berries attract birds. Aphid, thrip, spider mite susceptible.

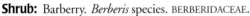

Shrub: Azalea. *Rhododendron* species. ERICACEAE.

Description: Over 10 species and many hybrids of slow-growing, spreading, mostly deciduous shrubs or small trees, 3–10 ft. (90–300 cm) tall, with waxy, bright green, oval leaves, to 4 in. (10 cm) long, in radiating clusters.

Blooms/Berries: Fragrant, trumpet-shaped, cream, orange, pink, red, white, or yellow flowers in spring–summer, to 2 in. (50 mm) wide, in clusters.

Plant hardiness: Zones 4–9. Ground hardy zones 7–9.

Soil: Moist, well-drained. Fertility: Rich. 6.0–6.5 pH.

Planting: Filtered sun–full shade. Space 4 ft. (1.2 m) apart.

Care: Moderate. Keep moist until established; reduce watering thereafter. Fertilize monthly spring–autumn. Avoid cultivating around plants. Propagate by cuttings, layering. Protect from sun in hot climates.

Features: Good choice for woodland gardens. Good autumn color. Powdery mildew susceptible.

Shrub: Barberry. *Berberis* species. BERBERIDACEAE.

Description: About 500 species of medium-growth, spiny, dense, deciduous or evergreen shrubs, 4–8 ft. (1.2–2.4 m) tall, depending on species, with shiny, hollylike, green, red, yellow, or variegated leaves, 1–3 in. (25–75 mm) long, turning red, purple in autumn.

Blooms/Berries: Many cup-shaped, bright yellow to red flowers in spring, forming hanging branched clusters, 1–4 in. (25–100 mm) long, with black, blue, red, yellow berries in autumn.

Plant hardiness: Zones 3–9, depending on species.

Soil: Dry–moist, well-drained. Fertility: Average–low. 5.0–7.0 pH.

Planting: Full sun–partial shade. Space 2–6 ft. (60–180 cm) apart, depending on species and use.

Care: Easy. Allow surface soil to dry between waterings until established. Fertilize annually in spring. Prune by removing oldest wood. Protect from sun, wind. Propagate by cuttings, layering, seed.

Features: Good choice for accents, barriers, hedges in arid, small-space, woodland gardens and landscapes. Flowers, berries attract birds, hummingbirds. Drought, humidity, smog tolerant. Some species regulated to prevent stem rust disease.

Shrub: Bayberry, Northern; Swamp Candleberry. *Myrica pensylvanica.* MYRICACEAE.

Description: Medium-growth, dense, spreading, deciduous to semi-evergreen shrub, to 9 ft. (2.7 m) tall, with waxy, yellow green, broad, oval leaves, to 4 in. (10 cm) long, often with conspicuous wax secretions.

Blooms/Fruit: Inconspicuous white flowers form small, gray, wax-coated berrylike fruit in autumn, persisting to winter.

Plant hardiness: Zones 2–9. Ground hardy zones 5–8.

Soil: Dry–moist, well-drained. Fertility: Average–low. 5.5–7.5 pH.

Planting: Full sun–partial shade. Space 5–7 ft. (1.5–2.1 m) apart.

Care: Easy. Allow surface soil to dry between waterings until established. Fertilize annually in spring. Prune to maintain size and dense habit. Propagate by layering, seed.

Features: Good choice for borders, hedges, mass plantings in landscapes. Fruit attracts birds. Drought, salt, shade, wind tolerant. Disease, pest resistant. Source of aromatic bayberry wax.

Shrub: Beauty Bush. *Kolkwitzia amabilis.* CAPRIFOLIACEAE.
Description: Fast-growing, arching, deciduous, herbaceous shrub, to 15 ft. (4.5 m) tall and wide, with gray green, oval leaves, to 3 in. (75 mm) long, sometimes turning red in autumn, and with brown, flaking bark.
Blooms/Fruit: Showy, five-petaled, pink flowers with bristly, yellow centers in late spring, to ½ in. (12 mm) long, forming dense clusters, with distinctive, bristly, brown fruit in summer. Blooms on second-year wood.
Plant hardiness: Zones 4–9. Ground hardy zones 6–8.
Soil: Moist, well-drained. Fertility: Rich–low. 6.0–8.0 pH.
Planting: Full sun–partial shade. Space 12 ft. (3.5 m) apart.
Care: Easy. Keep moist. Fertilize monthly spring–summer. Mulch, zones 4–5. Prune after bloom. Protect from sun in hot climates. Propagate by cuttings.
Features: Good choice for backgrounds, borders, fences in woodland gardens. Fruit attracts birds. Disease, pest resistant.

Shrub: Boxwood. *Buxus* species. BUXACEAE.
Description: About 30 species of slow-growing, compact, dense, evergreen shrubs, to 6 ft. (1.8 m) tall and wide, with shiny, midgreen, round leaves, ½–1 in. (12–25 mm) long. Dwarf varieties available.
Blooms/Berries: Tiny, white flowers in spring, in clusters borne at junction of leaf with limb, form berry- or caplike fruit in summer.
Plant hardiness: Zones 5–9. Ground hardy zones 6–9.
Soil: Moist, well-drained humus. Fertility: Rich. 6.0–7.5 pH.
Planting: Full sun–partial shade. Space 1 ft. (30 cm) apart for hedges, 3 ft. (90 cm) apart for landscape plants, depending on species.
Care: Easy. Keep evenly moist. Fertilize quarterly in spring–autumn. Avoid cultivating around plants. Prune and shear in spring, autumn. Mulch, zones 8–9. Protect from wind.
Features: Good choice for backgrounds, edgings, hedges, paths, topiary in cottage, formal, natural, small-space gardens and landscapes. Best in mild climates. Scale, spider mite susceptible.

Shrub: Broom. *Cytisus* species. FABACEAE (LEGUMINOSAE).
Description: About 50 species of fast-growing, spreading, deciduous or semi-evergreen shrubs, 8–180 in. (20–450 cm) tall, depending on species, usually with three-part, divided or sometimes single, green leaves, ½–4 in. (12–100 mm) long.
Blooms/Seed: Fragrant, pealike, brown, red, white, yellow flowers in late spring, to 1 in. (25 mm) long, often in pairs or showy clusters, form beanlike seedpods in summer.
Plant hardiness: Zones 2–9, depending on species. Ground hardy zones 6–8.
Soil: Dry–damp, well-drained. Fertility: Average–low. 6.5–7.5 pH.
Planting: Full sun. Space 1–8 ft. (30–240 cm) apart, depending on species.
Care: Easy. Allow surface soil to dry between waterings until established. Fertilize semi-annually in spring, autumn. Mulch, zones 2–5, 8–9. Prune after bloom. Protect from sun in hot climates. Propagate by cuttings, grafting, layering, seed.
Features: Good choice for accents, borders, hedges, screens in cottage, small-space, seaside gardens. Salt tolerant. Humidity susceptible. Some species are very invasive.

Shrub: Burning Bush; Wahoo. *Euonymus atropupurea.* CELASTRACEAE.

Description: Several cultivars of medium- to slow-growing, mounding, dense, deciduous small trees, to 25 ft. (7.5 m) tall, with shiny, bronze to green or variegated, broad, lance-shaped, pointed, finely toothed leaves, to 5 in. (13 cm) long, turning bright red in autumn.

Blooms/Fruit: Inconspicuous, fragrant, pink flowers in spring form red, caplike, woody fruit, bearing seed in autumn.

Plant hardiness: Zones 3–10. Ground hardy zones 4–9.

Soil: Dry–damp, well-drained. Fertility: Average. 6.0–8.0 pH.

Planting: Full sun. Space 10–12 ft. (3.0–3.7 m) apart.

Care: Easy. Allow surface soil to dry between waterings until established. Fertilize quarterly spring–autumn. Mulch, zones 3, 10. Prune sparingly after bloom. Protect from sun in hot climates. Propagate by cuttings, layering, seed.

Features: Good choice for accents, borders, groups in formal, small-space, woodland gardens. Seed attracts birds. Drought, salt tolerant. Mildew, scale susceptible.

> **Warning**
>
> Foliage of burning bush poses hazard of digestive upset if ingested. Avoid planting in gardens frequented by children or pets.

Shrub: Butterfly Bush. *Buddleia davidii.* BUDDLEIACEAE.

Description: Several cultivars of wide, willowlike, mostly deciduous shrubs, 4–15 ft. (1.2–4.5 m) tall with hairy or feltlike, gray green to dark green, narrow, pointed leaves, 3–5 in. (75–125 mm) long.

Blooms/Berries: Small, fragrant, lilaclike, orange, pink, purple, white, or yellow flowers in spring–summer form arching spikes to 10 in. (25 cm) long, with dry, berrylike seed pods in autumn.

Plant hardiness: Zones 5–10. Ground hardy zones 7–10.

Soil: Dry–moist, well-drained soils. Fertility: Average–low. 7.0 pH.

Planting: Full sun–partial shade. Space 3 ft. (90 cm) apart.

Care: Easy. Allow surface soil to dry between waterings. Fertilize monthly spring–winter. Deadhead. Prune in spring: to ground in cold-winter climates; one-third to ground in mild-winter climates. Propagate by cuttings, seed.

Features: Good choice for backgrounds, borders in arid, cottage, tropical gardens. Attracts bees, butterflies, hummingbirds.

Shrub: Camellia, Common. *Camellia japonica.* THEACEAE.

Description: Over 200 cultivars of slow-growing, bushy, evergreen shrubs or small trees, 6–45 ft. (1.8–14 m) tall with shiny or waxy, dark green, oval, smooth leaves, 2½–4 in. (65–100 mm) long. Popular cultivars include 'Adolphe Audusson', with red or variegated, semi-double flowers; 'Alba Plena', with white, double flowers; and 'Covina', with pink, red double flowers.

Blooms/Berries: Fragrant, pink, red, white, or multicolored, single, semi-double, or double flowers in late winter–spring, 2–9 in. (5–23 cm) wide.

Plant hardiness: Zones 6–10. Ground hardy zones 8–10.

Soil: Moist, well-drained. Fertility: Rich. 6.0–6.5 pH.

Planting: Partial shade. Space 4–5 ft. (1.2–1.5 m) apart.

Care: Easy. Keep evenly moist. Fertilize semi-monthly year round. Mulch. Prune after bloom. Protect from sun in hot climates, frost in zones 6–7. Propagate by cuttings.

Features: Good choice for accents, borders, containers, hedges, screen, walls, paths in cottage, formal, natural, shade, small-space, woodland gardens.

Shrub: Cinquefoil, Bush; Shrubby Cinquefoil. *Potentilla fruticosa.* ROSACEAE.
Description: Many cultivars of medium- to slow-growing, textured, dense, round, deciduous shrubs, 2–4 ft. (60–120 cm) tall, with shiny, light or dark green, oval- or lance-shaped, usually five-lobed, divided leaves, to ¾ in. (19 mm) long.
Blooms/Seed: Many, open, orange, pink, red, white, or yellow, long-lasting single flowers in spring–autumn, to 1¼ in. (32 mm) wide, form brown seed on female shrubs.
Plant hardiness: Zones 2–9. Hardy.
Soil: Moist–damp, well-drained. Fertility: Rich–low. 6.0–8.0 pH.
Planting: Full sun–partial shade. Space 3–4 ft. (90–120 cm) apart.
Care: Easy. Allow surface soil to dry between waterings until established. Fertilize quarterly spring–autumn. Mulch, zones 2–4. Prune after bloom. Protect from sun in hot climates. Propagate by division, seed.
Features: Good choice for backgrounds, beds, borders, edgings, hedges in cottage, formal, rock, small-space gardens. Drought tolerant. Disease resistant. Spider mite susceptible.

Shrub: Cotoneaster, Spreading. *Cotoneaster divaricatus.* ROSACEAE.
Description: Deciduous shrub, to 6 ft. (1.8 m) tall and 10 ft. (3 m) wide with shiny, dark green, smooth, oval, pointed leaves, to ¾ in. (19 mm) long. Branches bear thorny spurs.
Blooms/Berries: Pink or red flowers, to ½ in. (12 mm) wide in spring, form red berries in autumn–winter, ½ in. (12 mm) wide.
Plant hardiness: Zones 5–10. Ground hardy zones 7–9.
Soil: Moist, well-drained. Fertility: Average–low. 6.5–7.0 pH.
Planting: Partial shade. Space 5 ft. (1.5 m) apart.
Care: Easy. Allow surface soil to dry between waterings until established. Fertilize monthly spring–autumn. Minimal pruning. Protect from frost, zones 5–6. Propagate by cuttings, seed.
Features: Good choice for barriers, espalier, ground cover, hedges, paths in formal, natural, rock gardens. Good ground cover for erosion control on hillsides. Berries attract birds. Drought, salt, wind tolerant.

Shrub: Cranberry Bush, European; Whitten Tree. *Viburnum opulus.* CAPRIFOLIACEAE.
Description: Several cultivars of graceful, medium-growth, open, deciduous shrubs, to 12 ft. (3.7 m) tall, with veined, maplelike, three- to five-lobed, divided leaves, to 4 in. (10 cm) long, turning bright red in autumn.
Blooms/Berries: Many showy, cream, white, single flowers in late spring, to ¾ in. (19 mm) wide, form mounding clusters, to 4 in. (10 cm) wide, with scarlet berries in autumn, persisting to winter.
Plant hardiness: Zones 3–10. Ground hardy zones 3–8.
Soil: Dry–moist, well-drained. Fertility: Rich–average. 6.0–7.5 pH.
Planting: Full sun–partial shade. Space 6–8 ft. (1.8–2.4 m) apart.
Care: Easy. Keep evenly moist. Fertilize quarterly spring–autumn. Mulch, zones 7–10. Prune after bloom. Protect from sun in hot climates. Propagate by cuttings, grafting, layers, seed.
Features: Good choice for accents, borders, margins, screens in cottage, natural, rock, water, woodland gardens. Berries attract birds. Disease resistant. Aphid, spider mite susceptible.

Shrub: Daphne. *Daphne* species. THYMELAEACEAE.

Description: About 50 species of slow-growing, compact or spreading, deciduous or evergreen shrubs, to 4 ft. (1.2 m) tall, with shiny, dark green or variegated, thick, oval, pointed leaves, 1–3 in. (25–75 mm) long.

Blooms/Fruit: Small, very fragrant, funnel-shaped, pink, purple, white, waxy, single flowers in late winter, form clusters to 4 in. (10 cm) long, with red fruit.

Plant hardiness: Zones 5–9, depending on species. Lilac daphne, *D. genkwa*, and winter daphne, *D. odora*, ground hardy zones 7–9; other species ground hardy zones 5–9.

Soil: Moist, well-drained humus. Fertility: Rich. 6.5–7.0 pH.

Planting: Partial shade. Space 3–5 ft. (90–150 cm) apart. Set plant 1 in. (25 mm) above surrounding soil.

Care: Moderate–complex. Allow surface soil to dry between waterings until established. Fertilize annually in winter. Mulch. Prune after bloom. Protect from sun, wind in hot climates. Propagate by cuttings, grafting, layering, seed.

Features: Good choice for borders, containers, cutting, edging, paths in cottage, small-space, woodland gardens. Good corsage flower. Aphid susceptible. Disease resistant.

> **Warning**
>
> All parts of daphne are hazardous if ingested. Avoid planting in gardens frequented by children or pets.

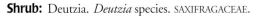

Shrub: Deutzia. *Deutzia* species. SAXIFRAGACEAE.

Description: About 40 species of medium- to slow-growing, mounded or arching, usually deciduous shrubs, 6–9 ft. (1.8–2.7 m) tall, with smooth, green, lance-shaped, pointed, finely toothed leaves, 2–5 in. (50–125 mm) long. Dwarf species available. Some species have attractive, reddish brown bark.

Blooms/Seed: Small, star-shaped, pink, purple, white, simple flowers in late spring, to 1 in. (25 mm) wide, in arching clusters, form many small seeds.

Plant hardiness: Zones 4–9, depending on species. Most species ground hardy zones 6–9.

Soil: Moist, well-drained. Fertility: Average. 6.0–7.5 pH.

Planting: Full sun–partial shade. Space 5–7 ft. (1.5–2.1 m) apart.

Care: Easy. Keep moist. Fertilize quarterly spring–autumn. Prune after bloom. Protect from frost. Propagate by cuttings, division, layering, seed.

Features: Good choice for background, border, hedges, mixed plantings in cottage, natural, woodland gardens. Pest, disease resistant.

Shrub: Enkianthus, Redvein. *Enkianthus campanulatus*. ERICACEAE.

Description: Several cultivars of slow-growing, dense, spreading, layered, deciduous small trees, to 30 ft. (9 m) tall, with shiny, dark green, oval or lance-shaped, pointed, toothed leaves, to 3 in. (75 mm) long, turning red in autumn.

Blooms/Berries: Small, bell-shaped, orange, yellow, red-veined, flowers in spring, form abundant, hanging clusters with caplike fruit in autumn.

Plant hardiness: Zones 5–9. Ground hardy zones 6–8.

Soil: Dry–moist, well-drained. Fertility: Rich. 6.0–6.5 pH.

Planting: Full sun–partial shade. Space 10–12 ft. (3.0–3.7 m) apart.

Care: Easy. Keep evenly moist. Fertilize quarterly spring–autumn. Mulch. Limit pruning. Propagate by cuttings, layering, seed.

Features: Good choice for accents, borders, mixed plantings in natural, shade, woodland gardens. Salt susceptible. Pest, disease resistant.

Shrub: Fatsia, Japanese; Japanese Aralia; Formosa Rice Tree. *Fatsia japonica (Aralia sieboldii)*. ARALIACEAE.

Description: Several cultivars of medium-growth, tropical-like, open, evergreen shrub, to 20 ft. (6 m) high and wide, with shiny, deep green or variegated, 7- to 11-lobed leaves, to 16 in. (40 cm) wide. Branches and trunk are marked with light, crescent-shaped scars.

Blooms/Fruit: Many tiny white flowers in autumn, in open, dangling clusters, to 18 in. (45 cm) long, form black, round, berrylike fruit, persisting through winter.

Plant hardiness: Zones 7–10. Ground hardy zones 8–10.

Soil: Moist, well-drained loam. Fertility: Rich–average. 6.0–6.5 pH.

Planting: Partial–full shade. Space 4–6 ft. (1.2–1.8 m) apart.

Care: Moderate. Keep evenly moist. Fertilize monthly spring–autumn. Mulch. Prune to shape in spring. Remove suckers. Protect from sun, wind in hot climates.

Features: Good choice for accents, backgrounds, containers, fences, screens in indoor, small-space, tropical gardens. Slug, snail susceptible.

Shrub: Firethorn; Pyracantha. *Pyracantha* species. ROSACEAE.

Description: About six species of medium-growth, upright or spreading, dense, evergreen, thorny shrubs, 6–20 ft. (1.8–6.0 m) tall, depending on species, with shiny or leathery, green, lance-shaped leaves, ¾–4 in. (19–100 mm) long. Common species include *P. coccinea* and *P. crenotoserrata*.

Blooms/Berries: Many small white flowers in spring, in dense, mounding clusters, form bright red berries in autumn, persisting to winter.

Plant hardiness: Zones 4–9, depending on species. All species ground hardy zones 7–9.

Soil: Moist, well-drained. Fertility: Average. 6.0–8.0 pH.

Planting: Full sun. Space 6–8 ft. (1.8–2.4 m) apart.

Care: Moderate. Allow surface soil to dry between waterings until established. Fertilize annually in spring. Prune after bloom, using care to avoid sharp thorns. Propagate by cuttings, grafting, layering, seed.

Features: Good choice for accent, barrier, espalier, ground cover in arid, formal, small-space, wildlife gardens. Best in dry climates. Berries attract birds. Avoid transplanting. Apple scab, fireblight susceptible.

Shrub: Forsythia. *Forsythia* × *intermedia*. OLEACEAE.

Description: Many hybrids and cultivars of dainty, fast-growing, arching, open, deciduous shrubs, to 10 ft. (3 m) tall, with bright green, simple, sometimes three-lobed, oval, pointed leaves, to 5 in. (13 cm) long.

Blooms/Seed: Many yellow flowers in spring, to 1 in. (25 mm) long, in showy clusters along arched branches, form winged seed in autumn. Flowers appear before leaves, on second-year wood.

Plant hardiness: Zones 4–8.

Soil: Moist, average loam. Fertility: Average. 6.5–8.0 pH.

Planting: Full sun. Space 8–10 ft. (2.4–3.0 m) apart.

Care: Easy. Keep moist. Fertilize quarterly spring–autumn. Mulch, zones 4–6. Prune by thinning oldest canelike stems after bloom. Propagate by cuttings, layering, seed.

Features: Good choice for backgrounds, borders, cutting, hedges, mixed plantings in natural, woodland gardens. Good for indoor floral display.

Shrub: Fothergilla, Dwarf; Witch Alder. *Fothergilla gardenii.*
HAMAMELIDACEAE.

Description: Medium- to slow-growing, bushy, mounding, deciduous shrub, to 4 ft. (1.2 m) tall, with deep green or blue green, oval, pointed leaves, 1–2 in. (25–50 mm) long, turning orange, red, yellow, variegated in autumn.

Blooms/Fruit: Tiny, filament-like, white flowers in spring, form round, upright, bottle-brush-like clusters, to 2 in. (50 mm) long, with caplike fruit in summer. Flowers usually appear before leaves.

Plant hardiness: Zones 4–9. Ground hardy zones 5–9.

Soil: Moist, well-drained. Add acidic compost or leaf mold. Fertility: Rich–average. 5.5–6.5 pH.

Planting: Full sun–partial shade. Space 3–4 ft. (90–120 cm) apart.

Care: Easy. Allow surface soil to dry between waterings until established. Fertilize annually in spring. Mulch, zones 4–6. Prune after bloom. Propagate by cuttings, layering, seed.

Features: Good choice for accents, backgrounds, beds, borders, cutting in cottage, woodland gardens. Blooms best in full sun. Pest, disease resistant.

Shrub: Gardenia, Common; Cape Jessamine. *Gardenia jasminoides.*
RUBIACEAE.

Description: Slow-growing, bushy, evergreen shrub, to 6 ft. (1.8 m) tall, with shiny, dark green, oval, veined, pointed, thick leaves, 3–4 in. (75–100 mm) long.

Blooms/Berries: Very fragrant, yellow or white, often double flowers 2–3 ½ in. wide (50–90 mm) wide, in autumn–winter.

Plant hardiness: Zones 8–11.

Soil: Moist, well-drained. Fertility: Average. Add acidic compost or leaf mold. 4.5–5.5 pH.

Planting: Partial shade. 2–3 ft. (60–90 cm) apart.

Care: Moderate. Keep evenly moist. Limit watering in summer. Fertilize in spring. Pinch off buds until early autumn. Deadhead blooms and suckers. Prune after bloom. Protect from sun in hot climates, frost in zone 8. Propagate by cuttings.

Features: Best for containers, cutting, informal hedges, pathways in cutting, rock, water gardens. Aphid, mealybug, scale, spider mite susceptible.

Shrub: Gold-Dust Plant; Japanese Laurel. *Aucuba japonica.* CORNACEAE.

Description: Bushy, dense, evergreen shrub, to 15 ft. (4.5 m) tall, with glossy, dark green and variegated, oval, toothed leaves, 4–7 in. (10–18 cm) long.

Blooms/Berries: Tiny purple flowers in spring, with scarlet, berry-like fruit in autumn, to ½ in. (12 mm) wide, in clusters.

Plant hardiness: Zones 7–11. Tender.

Soil: Dry–moist, well-drained. Fertility: Rich–average. 6.0–8.0 pH.

Planting: Full sun–partial shade. Space 3 ft. (90 cm) apart.

Care: Easy. Allow surface soil to dry between waterings until established. Fertilize every 3–4 months year round. Prune winter–early spring. Protect from sun in hot climates. Propagate by cuttings, seed.

Features: Good choice for accents, containers, edgings, fences in indoor, shade, small-space, formal gardens. Drought, salt, smog tolerant. Mealybug, spider mite susceptible.

Shrub: Hazel, Winter. *Corylopsis* species. HAMAMELIDACEAE.

Description: About 10 species of graceful, slow-growing, spreading, open, deciduous shrubs, 6–20 ft. (1.8–6.0 m) tall, depending on species, with red-tinged buds turning to smooth, bright green, broad, oval, pointed, toothed leaves, to 4 in. (10 cm) long, turning yellow in autumn.

Blooms/Seed: Many yellow, bell- or tube-shaped flowers in spring, to ¾ in. (19 mm) long, form small, dangling clusters, with caplike seedpods in summer. Flowers appear before leaves.

Plant hardiness: Zones 4–9, depending on species. Ground hardy zones 7–9.

Soil: Moist, well-drained. Fertility: Rich. Add acidic leaf mold. 5.5–6.5 pH.

Planting: Full sun–partial shade. Space 6–10 ft. (1.8–3.0 m) apart, depending on species.

Care: Easy. Keep evenly moist. Fertilize annually in spring. Mulch, zones 4–6. Prune after bloom. Protect from sun in hot climates, wind and frost in zones 4–7. Propagate by cuttings, division, layering, seed.

Features: Good choice for backgrounds, borders, walls in cottage, natural, woodland gardens. Disease and pest resistant.

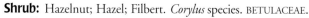

Shrub: Hazelnut; Hazel; Filbert. *Corylus* species. BETULACEAE.

Description: About 10 species of slow-growing, spreading, deciduous shrubs or trees, 10–120 ft. (3–37 m) tall depending on species, with smooth, alderlike, yellow green, fuzzy, oval, pointed, toothed leaves, usually 4–6 in. (10–15 cm) long, turning yellow in autumn. Harry Lauder's Walking Stick, *C. avellana* 'Contorta', has distinctive twisted trunk and limbs.

Blooms/Nuts: Inconspicuous female flowers and long, dangling, willowlike male catkins borne on same tree in spring, form edible nuts in autumn.

Plant hardiness: Zones 5–9. Ground hardy zones 6–8.

Soil: Damp, well-drained. Fertility: Average. 6.0–8.0 pH.

Planting: Full sun–partial shade. Space 8–12 ft. (2.4–3.7 m) apart.

Care: Easy. Allow surface soil to dry between waterings until established. Fertilize quarterly spring–autumn. Remove all suckers. Prune autumn. Propagate by cuttings, grafting, nuts.

Features: Good choice for accent, backgrounds, edgings, screens in cottage, woodland gardens. Some species regulated to prevent Eastern filbert blight.

Shrub: Heath. *Erica* species. ERICACEAE.

Description: Over 500 species of slow-growing, branching or spreading, evergreen shrubs or small trees, usually 1–6 ft. (30–180 cm) tall, with tiny, heatherlike needles or leaves. Scotch heather, *Calluna vulgaris*, is a close relative with similar care needs. Dwarf and ground cover species available.

Blooms/Seed: Abundant, tiny, green, rose, purple, white, yellow flowers in late winter–early spring, with seedy caps in summer.

Plant hardiness: Zones 5–10, depending on species.

Soil: Damp, well-drained humus. Fertility: Rich. 5.5–6.5 pH.

Planting: Full sun. Space 3 ft. (90 cm) apart.

Care: Easy. Allow surface soil to dry between waterings until established. Fertilize annually in spring. Prune or shear after bloom. Protect from sun in hot climates. Propagate by cuttings, seed.

Features: Good choice for borders, edgings in arid, rock gardens.

Shrub: Heather, Scotch. *Calluna vulgaris.* ERICACEAE.

Description: Many cultivars of slow-growing, mounding or spreading, evergreen shrubs, to 3 ft. (90 cm) tall, with small, overlapped, green, maroon, yellow, scaly leaves, tinged bronze or red in autumn.

Blooms/Seed: Tiny pink, purple, white, trumpet-shaped, double flowers in summer, in upright spikes, to 10 in. (25 cm) long, with caplike seedpods.

Plant hardiness: Zones 5–7.

Soil: Moist, well-drained loam. Fertility: Rich–average. 5.5–6.5 pH.

Planting: Full sun–partial shade. Space 3 ft. (90 cm) apart.

Care: Easy. Keep moist. Fertilize semi-annually spring and autumn. Mulch. Prune or shear after bloom. Protect from sun, wind in hot climates. Propagate by cuttings, seed.

Features: Good choice for borders, edgings, ground covers, mixed plantings in cottage, rock, small-space, woodland gardens. Best in cool, moist climates. Heat, humidity susceptible.

Shrub: Heavenly Bamboo. *Nandina domestica.* BERBERIDACEAE.

Description: Bushy, loose, evergreen shrub, to 8 ft. (2.4 m) tall and 4 ft. (1.2 m) wide, with bamboolike, delicate, light green, oval, pointed leaves, 2 in. (50 mm) long, tinted bronze or yellow in some cultivars, turning red in autumn. Dwarf cultivars to 1 ft. (30 cm) tall and 1 ft. (30 cm) wide.

Blooms/Berries: Small white flowers in late spring–summer, in lacy clusters to 1 ft. (30 cm) long, with red berries in autumn to ¼ in. (6 mm) wide.

Plant hardiness: Zones 6–10. Ground hardy zones 7–10.

Soil: Dry–moist, well-drained. Fertility: Rich–average. 6.5–7.0 pH.

Planting: Full sun–partial shade. Space 2–6 ft. (60–180 cm) apart, depending on cultivar.

Care: Easy. Allow surface soil to dry between waterings until established. Fertilize semi-monthly spring–autumn. Prune early spring. Mulch, zones 6–7. Protect from frost, zone 6. Propagate by seed.

Features: Good choice for containers, screen in tropical gardens. Berries more abundant if groups are planted. Drought tolerant. Deer-resistant.

Shrub: Holly. *Ilex* species. AQUIFOLIACEAE.

Description: Nearly 400 species of medium- to slow-growing, rounded, dense, mostly evergreen shrubs or small trees, 10–50 ft. (3–15 m) tall depending on species, with shiny, leathery, deep green, toothed, usually spiny leaves, to 4 in. (10 cm) long.

Blooms/Berries: Inconspicuous white or green flowers form round, black or red berries on female trees, in clusters, to 6 in. (15 cm) long, in autumn. Plant a pollinating male tree with one or more female trees.

Plant hardiness: Zones 4–8, depending on species. Ground hardy zones 7–8.

Soil: Moist, well-drained. Fertility: Average. 6.0–7.0 pH.

Planting: Full sun–partial shade. Space 8–12 ft. (2.4–3.7 m) apart, depending on species.

Care: Moderate. Keep moist. Fertilize annually in spring. Mulch. Prune spring. Protect from sun, wind in hot climates. Propagate by cuttings, grafting, seed.

Features: Good choice for accents, borders, backgrounds, hedges in cottage, formal, small-space gardens. Berries attract birds. Mealbug, leaf miner, scale susceptible.

Shrub: Honeysuckle, Tatarian. *Lonicera tatarica.* CAPRIOFOLIACEAE.
Description: Over 12 cultivars of tall and arching, deciduous shrubs, to 10 ft. (3 m) tall, with dull, green to blue green, oval or lance-shaped leaves, to 2½ in. (65 mm) long, turning bronze in autumn.
Blooms/Berries: Dainty, fragrant, fuchsialike, coral, pink, white, yellow, tubular, nectar-bearing flowers in spring, 1 in. (25 mm) wide, form red berries in late spring–summer.
Plant hardiness: Zones 5–9.
Soil: Moist, well-drained. Fertility: Average. 6.0–6.5 pH.
Planting: Full sun–partial shade. Space 7 ft. (2 m) apart.
Care: Easy. Allow surface soil to dry between waterings until established. Fertilize monthly spring–autumn. Prune after bloom. Propagate by cuttings, layering, seed.
Features: Good choice for fences, ground covers, hedges, trellises in natural, cottage gardens. Attracts bees, hummingbirds. Invasive. Ant, aphid susceptible.

Shrub: Hydrangea. *Hydrangea* species. HYDRANGEACEAE (SAXIFRAGACEAE).
Description: Over 20 species of tall or climbing, bushy, deciduous or evergreen shrubs, 4–8 ft. (1.2–2.4 m) tall, with shiny, dark green, broad, oval, lobed or deeply toothed leaves, to 1 ft. (30 cm) long.
Blooms/Seed: Abundant blue, lavender, pink, purple, white, round or star-shaped, sometimes sterile flowers in summer–early autumn, to 1 in. (25 mm) wide, form mounding clusters, to 18 in. (45 cm) wide, with seed in autumn.
Plant hardiness: Zones 4–10. Most ground hardy zones 6–10.
Soil: Moist, well-drained, loose. Add compost or leaf mold. 6.5–7.0 pH. For best blue flowers, add aluminum sulfate; reds and pinks, garden lime.
Planting: Full sun–partial shade. Space 6–10 ft. (1.8–3 m) apart.
Care: Moderate. Allow surface soil to dry between waterings until established. Fertilize semi-monthly spring–summer. Deadhead. Prune severely in autumn or early spring. Propagate by cuttings, division, layering, seed.
Features: Good choice for borders, hedges, screens in cottage, woodland gardens. Cut and dry flower heads for wreaths and floral arrangements. Aphid and chlorosis, mildew susceptible.

Shrub: Juniper, Common. *Juniperus communis.* CUPRESSACEAE.
Description: Many cultivars of very diverse, medium- to slow-growing, erect, prostrate, or spreading, dense, evergreen, coniferous shrubs and small trees, 2–35 ft. (60 cm–10 m) tall, depending on cultivar, with shiny green needles that mature to scaly, cedarlike foliage. Columnar, ground cover, tree, and shrub habits are available in various cultivars.
Blooms/Cones: Male, yellow, catkinlike cones and female, blue or black, aromatic, pulpy, berrylike cones appear in spring, ripening in autumn.
Plant hardiness: Zones 2–9. Very hardy.
Soil: Dry to damp, well-drained loam. Fertility: Average. 5.5–8.0 pH.
Planting: Full sun–partial shade. Space varies by cultivar.
Care: Easy. Allow surface soil to dry between waterings until established. Fertilize annually in spring. Prune only to shape new growth. Propagate by cuttings, grafting, seed.
Features: Good choice for accents, borders, edgings, ground covers, hedges, screens, topiary in formal, small-space, woodland gardens and landscapes. Aphid, borer, spider mite and juniper blight susceptible.

Shrub: Laurel, Mountain; Calico Bush. *Kalmia latifolia.* ERICACEAE.

Description: Several cultivars of slow-growing, dense, mounding evergreen shrubs, to 10 ft. (3 m) tall, with shiny, azalea-like, deep green, leathery, lance-shaped, pointed leaves, to 5 in. (13 cm) long, and tinged orange red in autumn.

Blooms/Berries: Showy, cuplike, star-pointed, chocolate, pink, red, rose, white flowers in late spring, to 1½ in. (38 mm) wide, in mounding clusters, to 8 in. (20 cm) wide, with capsulelike seedpods in late summer. Flowers on second-year wood.

Plant hardiness: Zones 4–9. Ground hardy zones 5–8.

Soil: Moist, well-drained humus. Add acidic compost or leaf mold. 5.5–6.5 pH.

Planting: Full sun–full shade. Space 6–8 ft. (1.8–2.4 m) apart.

Care: Easy. Keep evenly moist. Fertilize quarterly spring–autumn. Mulch. Prune lightly after bloom. Protect from sun in hot climates. Propagate by cuttings, layering, seed.

Features: Good choice for backgrounds, mixed plantings, screens in natural, woodland gardens. Best planted with azalea, camellia, daphne, rhododendron.

Warning

Foliage of mountain laurel can cause severe digestive upset if ingested. Avoid planting in gardens frequented by children or pets.

Shrub: Lilac. *Syringa* species. OLEACEAE.

Description: Over 30 species of fast-growing, spreading, dense, deciduous shrubs, 5–20 ft. (1.5–6.0 m) tall, with shiny, dark green, smooth, oval leaves, to 5 in. (13 cm) long.

Blooms/Berries: Fragrant, tiny lavender, pink, purple, white flowers in spring forming large showy clusters, 3½–10 in. (9–25 cm) long, with leathery seed-filled capsules in summer. First blooms 2–3 years after planting. Requires winter chilling to bloom reliably.

Plant hardiness: Zones 3–9. Hardy.

Soil: Moist, well-drained. Fertility: Rich. 7.0–7.5 pH.

Planting: Full sun–partial shade. Space 5–10 ft. (1.5–3 m) apart.

Care: Moderate. Keep evenly moist. Fertilize quarterly spring–autumn. Deadhead. Prune sparingly after bloom. Propagate by cuttings, layering.

Features: Good choice for borders, cutting in cottage, woodland gardens. Attracts butterflies. Transplants readily. Invasive. Deer resistant. Powdery mildew susceptible.

Shrub: Mahonia. *Mahonia* species. BERBERIDACEAE.

Description: Over 100 species of slow-growing, spreading, broad-leaved, evergreen shrubs, to 12 ft. (3.7 m) tall depending on species, with shiny, blue green, leathery, toothed, usually spiny leaves, to 3 in. (75 mm) long, arranged along the stem in groups of five or seven, and tinged red in autumn.

Blooms/Fruit: Tiny, fragrant, yellow, bell-shaped flowers in spring, to ½ in. (12 mm) wide, in narrow spiking clusters, form blue, blueberry-like, mealy fruit in autumn.

Plant hardiness: Zones 4–8, depending on species.

Soil: Moist, well-drained humus. Fertility: Rich. 5.5–6.5 pH.

Planting: Partial–full shade. Space 5–7 ft. (1.5–2.1 m) apart.

Care: Easy–moderate. Keep evenly moist. Fertilize quarterly spring–autumn. Mulch, zones 7–8. Avoid pruning. Propagate by cuttings, layering, seed.

Features: Good choice for accents, background, barriers, fences, hedges in natural, woodland gardens. Fruit attracts birds. *M. aquifolium* drought tolerant. Pest, disease resistant.

Shrub: Mock Orange, Sweet. *Philadelphus coronarius.*
HYDRANGEACEAE (PHILADELPHACEAE).
Description: Many cultivars of fast-growing, dense, spreading, deciduous shrubs, to 10 ft. (3 m) tall and wide, with dull to shiny, green, oval, pointed leaves, 1–3 in. (25–75 mm) long.
Blooms/Seed: Very fragrant, creamy white flowers in late spring, to 1½ in. (38 mm) wide, in radiating clusters, form abundant seed in late summer.
Plant hardiness: Zones 5–9.
Soil: Moist, well-drained. Fertility: Rich–average. Add compost or leaf mold. 6.5–7.5 pH.
Planting: Partial shade. Space 3 ft. (90 cm) apart.
Care: Easy. Generally care free. Allow surface soil to dry between waterings until established. Fertilize semi-monthly spring–autumn. Prune after bloom. Propagate by cuttings, layers, seed.
Features: Good for borders, edgings, hedges, paths in formal, small-space, woodland gardens. Generally drought tolerant. Pest and disease resistant.

Shrub: Oleander, Common. *Nerium oleander.* APOCYNACEAE.
Description: Many cultivars of fast-growing, dense, bushy and arching, evergreen shrubs, to 20 ft. (6 m) tall and 12 ft. (3.7 m) wide, with dull, green, leathery, narrow leaves, to 1 ft. (30 cm) long.

Warning

All parts and sap of oleander pose severe hazard if ingested. Avoid planting in gardens frequented by children or pets.

Blooms/Seed: Mostly fragrant, pink, red, white, yellow, double or single flowers in spring–autumn, 2–3 in. (50–75 mm) wide, in showy clusters, form hairy, tufted seed in autumn.
Plant hardiness: Zones 8–11.
Soil: Moist. Fertility: Average–low. 6.5–7.0 pH.
Planting: Full sun. 5–10 ft. (1.5–3 m) apart.
Care: Easy. Generally care free. Allow surface soil to dry between waterings until established. Fertilize annually in spring. Mulch, zone 8. Prune after bloom. Prune heavily in cold-winter climates. Propagate by cuttings.
Features: Good choice for borders, containers, hedges, screens along driveways. Best in heat. So tough, used as freeway planting. Attractive all seasons. Fire retardant. Drought tolerant. Deer, rodent resistant. Aphid, scale susceptible.

Shrub: Oleaster; Wild Olive; Russian Olive; Silver Berry. *Elaeagnus angustifolia.* ELEAGNACEAE.
Description: Several varieties of fast-growing, spreading, often spiny, deciduous small trees, to 20 ft. (6 m) tall, with dull, olivelike, green, oval, pointed leaves, to 2 in. (50 mm) long, with silver undersides, and with brown, flaking bark.
Blooms/Fruit: Fragrant, fluted, bell-shaped, yellow green flowers in early spring, to ½ in. (12 mm) long, in clusters at leaf axils, with olivelike, mealy, red, silver, yellow fruit on short stalks in autumn.
Plant hardiness: Zones 3–8. Hardy.
Soil: Damp, well-drained. Fertility: Average–low. 5.5–8.0 pH.
Planting: Full sun–partial shade. Space 12–14 ft. (3.7–4.3 m) apart.
Care: Easy. Allow surface soil to dry between waterings until established. Fertilize annually in spring. Prune after bloom. Propagate by cuttings, grafting, layering, seed.
Features: Good choice for accents, barriers, espalier, hedges in landscapes. Drought tolerant.

Shrub: Pea Shrub, Siberian. *Caragana arborescens.* FABACEAE (LEGUMINOSAE).
Description: Several varieties of fast-growing, bushy, thorny, deciduous small trees, 6–20 ft. (1.8–6.0 m) tall, depending on variety, with shiny, yellow green, leaves, to 3 in. (75 mm) long, as three to six paired, oval leaflets.
Blooms/Seed: Showy, sweetpealike, yellow flowers in spring, to ⅞ in. (22 mm) long, in small clusters, with brown, bean- or pealike seedpods.
Plant hardiness: Zones 2–8. Hardy.
Soil: Moist, well-drained, sandy loam. Fertility: Average–poor. 6.5–8.5 pH.
Planting: Full sun. Space 5–6 ft. (1.5–1.8 m) apart.
Care: Easy. Allow surface soil to dry between waterings until established. Fertilize annually in spring. Prune after bloom. Propagate by cuttings, division, grafting, layering, seed.
Features: Good choice for accents, barriers, hedges, screens, windbreaks in arid, mountain, woodland gardens and landscapes. Drought tolerant. Deer, rodent and pest, disease resistant.

Shrub: Pine, Mountain; Mugo Pine. *Pinus mugo* var. *mugo.* PINACEAE.
Description: Several varieties and cultivars of slow-growing, usually mounding or spreading, sometimes upright, coniferous, evergreen shrubs or small trees, to 30 ft. (9 m) tall, with upright, bundled pairs of deep green needles, to 2 in. (50 mm) long.
Blooms/Cones: Male, yellow, catkinlike cones and female, brown, woody, clustered, flat-scaled cones appear in spring, ripening in autumn.
Plant hardiness: Zones 2–10. Hardy.
Soil: Damp, well-drained. Fertility: Average. 6.0–8.0 pH.
Planting: Full sun. Space 6–8 ft. (1.8–2.4 m) apart.
Care: Easy. Allow surface soil to dry between waterings until established. Avoid fertilizing. Shape growth by partial cutting of new growth "candles" in spring. Propagate by cuttings, grafting, seed.
Features: Good choice for accents, borders, containers, in formal, rock, small-space, woodland gardens. Good for bonsai, topiary. Spider mite, scale and chlorosis, rust susceptible.

Shrub: Pittosporum, Japanese; Mock Orange. *Pittosporum tobira.* PITTOSPORACEAE.
Description: Several cultivars of slow-growing, mounding, evergreen shrubs or small trees, to 18 ft. (5.5 m) tall, with shiny, green, yellow, variegated, leathery, oval leaves, to 4 in. (10 cm) long. Dwarf cultivar 'Wheeler's Dwarf' available.
Blooms/Fruit: Fragrant, bell-shaped, white flowers in spring, to ½ in. (12 mm) wide, in showy, mounded clusters, with attractive, round, orange, berrylike, seed-filled fruit in autumn.
Plant hardiness: Zones 7–10.
Soil: Damp, well-drained. Fertility: Average. 6.5–8.0 pH.
Planting: Full sun. Space 4–6 ft. (1.2–1.8 m) apart.
Care: Easy. Allow surface soil to dry between waterings until established. Mulch, zones 8–10. Prune in spring. Propagate by cuttings, grafting, seed.
Features: Good choice for backgrounds, beds, borders, hedges, edgings, paths in arid, Asian, cottage, small-space gardens and landscapes. Drought, humidity, salt tolerant. Aphid, scale susceptible.

Shrub: Privet; Hedge Plant. *Ligustrum* species. OLEACEAE.

Description: About 50 species of medium- to slow-growing, dense, bushy, deciduous or evergreen shrubs, 6–40 ft. (1.8–12.2 m) tall, depending on species, with shiny, green or gold, oval leaves, 1–4 in. (25–100 mm) long, and tinged russet or brown in autumn.

Blooms/Fruit: Abundant, fragrant, tiny, white flowers in late spring, in upright, grapelike clusters to 5 in. (13 cm) long, with black berrylike, seedy fruit in autumn.

Plant hardiness: Zones 4–10, depending on species.

Soil: Damp–moist, well-drained. Fertility: Rich–average. 6.0–8.0 pH.

Planting: Full sun–partial shade. Space according to use.

Care: Moderate. Keep damp. Fertilize quarterly spring–autumn. Mulch, zones 4–8. Protect tender species from frost in zones 4–7, sun in hot climates. Prune or shear after bloom. Propagate by cuttings, division, grafting, seed.

Features: Good choice for borders, containers, hedges, mass plantings, paths, walls in cottage, formal, small-space, woodland gardens and landscapes. Best in mild, cool climates. Fruit attracts birds. Pest, disease resistant.

Shrub: Quince, Japanese; Flowering Quince. *Chaenomeles speciosa.* ROSACEAE.

Description: Many cultivars of medium-growth, dense, branching or spreading, mostly spiny, semi-evergreen shrubs, 6–10 ft. (1.8–3.0 m) tall, with shiny, red turning deep green, oval, toothed leaves, to 3½ in. (90 mm) long, and tinged yellow in autumn.

Blooms/Fruit: Dainty, pink, red, white, single or double, waxy flowers in early spring before leaves appear, to 2½ in. (65 mm) wide, form showy clusters, sometimes with green, pear-shaped fruit in autumn.

Plant hardiness: Zones 5–9.

Soil: Damp–moist, well-drained. Fertility: Average. Add acidic compost or leaf mold. 5.5–6.5 pH.

Planting: Full sun. Space 5–6 ft. (1.5–1.8 m) apart.

Care: Easy. Allow surface soil to dry between waterings until established. Fertilize annually in spring. Prune after bloom. Propagate by cuttings, grafting, layering, seed.

Features: Good choice for barriers, bonsai, containers, cutting, walls in arid, Asian, cottage, woodland gardens. Smog tolerant. Chlorosis, leaf spot susceptible.

Shrub: Smoke Tree; Smokebush. *Cotinus coggygria.* ANARCARDIACEAE.

Description: Several cultivars of medium-growth, bushy, open, woody, deciduous shrubs, to 15 ft. (4.6 m) tall, with smooth, blue green or purple, oval, pointed leaves, to 3 in. (75 mm) long, turning red, purple in autumn.

Blooms/Seed: Tiny yellow flowers in early summer form dangling, branched clusters of lavender or purple, hairy "smoke," with small, berrylike, hard seed.

Plant hardiness: Zones 5–9.

Soil: Dry, well-drained. Fertility: Average–low. 6.0–8.0 pH.

Planting: Full sun. Space 15–20 ft. (4.5–6.0 m) apart.

Care: Easy. Allow surface soil to dry between waterings until established. Avoid fertilizing, pruning. Propagate by cuttings, layering, seed.

Features: Good choice for accents in arid, rock gardens. Drought, smog tolerant. American Smoke Tree, *C. obovatus*, is a related native species.

Shrub: Spirea, Vanhoutte. *Spiraea* x *vanhouttei*. ROSACEAE.
Description: Hybrid, fast-growing, arching, dense, deciduous shrub, to 6 ft. (1.8 m) tall, with red-tinged turning to blue green, slightly lobed, oval, veined leaves, to 1½ in. (38 mm) long, turning purple, red in autumn. Many other *Spiraea* species and cultivars available, some with summer blooms, requiring different care and pruning than does *S.* x *vanhouttei*.
Blooms/Seed: Tiny, fragrant, white flowers in spring, form showy, ball-shaped clusters, to 4 in. (10 cm) wide, along arched branches, with inconspicuous seed follicles in summer.
Plant hardiness: Zones 5–9.
Soil: Moist, well-drained. Fertility: Average. 6.0–8.0 pH.
Planting: Full sun–partial shade. Space 6–8 ft. (1.8–2.4 m) apart.
Care: Easy. Keep moist. Fertilize semi-annually spring and autumn. Prune after bloom, removing wood that has flowered. Propagate by cuttings, layering, seed.
Features: Good choice for accents, backgrounds, fences, hedges, walls in cottage, small-space, woodland gardens. Best in dry climates. Fireblight, powdery mildew susceptible.

Shrub: Weigela. *Weigela* species. CAPRIFOLIACEAE.
Description: Over 10 species and many hybrids of fast-growing, open, spreading, deciduous shrubs, to 10 ft. (3 m) tall, with shiny, dark green, oval, pointed leaves, to 4 in. (10 cm) long. Common species include *W. coraeensis* and *W. florida*, plus many named hybrids.
Blooms/Seed: Showy, cone-shaped, pink, purple, red, white, yellow flowers in late spring, to 1½ in. (38 mm) long), in dense clusters, form woody seedpods in summer. Flowers on second-year wood.
Plant hardiness: Zones 5–9.
Soil: Damp–moist, well-drained. Fertility: Average. 6.5–7.0 pH.
Planting: Full sun–partial shade. Space 8 ft. (2.4 m) apart.
Care: Easy. Keep evenly moist. Fertilize semi-monthly spring–autumn. Mulch. Prune after bloom. Propagate by cuttings.
Features: Good choice for accents, borders, flowers, hedges in cottage, woodland gardens. Pest resistant.

Shrub: Yew, American; Ground Hemlock. *Taxus canadensis*. TAXACEAE.
Description: Several cultivars of slow-growing, spreading, open, bushy, needle-bearing, evergreen shrubs, to 6 ft. (1.8 m) tall, with dark green, radiating, slightly flattened needles, to 1 in. (25 mm) long. Long-lived. English yew, *T. baccata*; and Japanese yew, *T. cuspidata* are related species.
Blooms/Fruit: Red, berrylike fruit in summer, to ½ in. (12 mm) wide, borne by female plants, form bony seedpods in autumn.
Plant hardiness: Zones 3–8. Best zones 3–6.
Soil needs: Well-drained. Fertility: Average. 7.0 pH.
Planting: Partial–full shade. Space 4–6 ft. (1.2–1.8 m) apart.
Care: Easy. Allow soil to completely dry between waterings. Fertilize annually in spring. Mulch. Avoid pruning. Protect from sun in hot climates, wind in cold-winter climates. Propagate by cuttings.
Features: Good choice for containers, hedges, screens in cottage, formal, shade, woodland gardens. Drought tolerant. Deer susceptible.

LANDSCAPE TREES

Tree: Alder. *Alnus* species. BETULACEAE.
Description: About 30 species of fast-growing, upright, open, deciduous trees, usually 60–80 ft. (18–24 m) tall, with shiny, heart-shaped or oval, deep green, finely toothed leaves, to 4 in. (10 cm) long, turning yellow in autumn. Cultivated species include American green alder, *A. crispa;* black alder, *A. glutinosa;* Italian alder, *A. cordata;* and white alder, *A. rhombifolia.* Dwarf species available.
Catkins/Cones: Willowlike catkins, to 3 in. (75 mm) long, in spring before leaves emerge, with brown, clustered cones, ½–1 in. (12–25 mm) long in autumn.
Plant hardiness: Zones 4–10, depending on species.
Soil: Moist, well-drained. Fertility: Average. 5.5–6.5 pH.
Planting: Full sun–full shade. Space 15–20 ft. (4.5–6 m) apart. Transplant in spring.
Care: Easy. Keep soil evenly moist. Prune to thin. Propagate by cuttings, seed.
Features: Good choice for margins, moist areas, understory in landscapes and water features. Very invasive. Shallow rooted. Borer, leaf miner, tent caterpillar and fungal disease susceptible.

Tree: Ash. *Fraxinus* species. OLEACEAE.
Description: About 65 species of fast-growing, spreading, mostly deciduous trees, 25–80 ft. (7.5–24 m) tall, with shiny, deep green to bronze, divided leaves, to 16 in. (40 cm) long, as 5–11 leaflets, turning purple, red in autumn. Cultivated species include European ash, *F. excelsior;* flowering ash, *F. ornus;* 'Raywood', *F. oxycarpa;* red ash, *F. pennsylvanica;* Texas ash, *F. texensis;* and white ash, *F. americana.*
Blooms/Seed: Inconspicuous, panicled flowers borne separately on male and female trees in spring. Maplelike seed in autumn. Seedless male cultivars available.
Plant hardiness: Varies by species; most are hardy in zones 7–10, some to zone 4.
Soil: Damp, well-drained. Fertility: Average–low. 6.5–8.0 pH.
Planting: Full sun. Space 15–20 ft. (4.5–6 m) apart. Transplant in spring.
Care: Easy. Keep soil damp. Prune to thin. Propagate by seed.
Features: Good choice for screens in arid, shade, woodland gardens and roadside plantings. Reduce maintenance by planting seedless cultivars. Drought tolerant. Anthracnose, borer, ash whitefly susceptible.

Tree: Beech. *Fagus* species. FAGACEAE.
Description: About 10 species of slow-growing, spreading or round-crowned, deciduous trees, to 100 ft. (30 m) tall, with shiny, green, oval, deeply veined, toothed leaves, 4–6 in. (10–15 cm) long, turning brown, yellow in autumn, and with smooth gray bark. Cultivated species include American beech, *F. grandifolia;* European beech, *F. sylvatica;* and Japanese beech, *F. crenata.*
Blooms/Seed: Inconspicuous flowers borne separately on male and female trees in spring. Bristle-covered seedpods bear beechnuts in autumn.
Plant hardiness: Zones 4–9. Best in cold-winter climates.
Soil: Well-drained. Fertility: Rich–average. 6.0–7.0 pH. Avoid transplanting.
Planting: Full sun–partial shade. Space 15–20 ft. (4.5–6.0 m) apart.
Care: Moderate. Allow surface soil to dry between waterings until established. Prune to remove pendulous branches and maintain high crown. Propagate by seed.
Features: Good choice for accents, allées in shade, woodland gardens, and roadside plantings. Leafburn susceptible in hot, dry climates. Pest, disease resistant.

Tree: Birch, Gray; White Birch; Fire Birch. *Betula populifolia.* BETULACEAE.
Description: Several cultivars of graceful, fast-growing, upright, open, deciduous trees, to 30 ft. (9 m) tall, with smooth, light green, triangular or diamond-shaped, toothed leaves, to 3 in. (75 mm) long, turning gold, yellow in autumn, and with white, flaking bark. Cultivars include 'Pendula', with drooping branches, and 'Purpurea', with purple-tinged foliage.
Catkins/Cones: Willowlike male and female catkins, to 2 in. (50 mm) long, in winter, with brown cones on female trees, to 1 in. (25 mm) long, in autumn.
Plant hardiness: Zones 4–7.
Soil: Moist, well-drained humus. Fertility: Rich–average. 5.5–7.0 pH.
Planting: Full–filtered sun. Space 12–15 ft. (3.7–4.5 m) apart.
Care: Easy. Keep moist. Prune in late spring. Propagate by cuttings, seed.
Features: Good choice for margins, moist areas in landscapes and water features. Tolerates occasional drought. Seed attracts birds in winter. Somewhat invasive. Shallow rooted. Aphid, birch leaf miner susceptible.

Tree: Birch, Paper; Canoe Birch, White Birch. *Betula papyrifera.* BETULACEAE.
Description: Over 10 cultivars of fast-growing, upright, graceful, short-lived, deciduous trees, to 100 ft. (30 m) tall with matte, light green, oval, pointed, finely toothed leaves, to 4 in. (10 cm) long, turning yellow in autumn. Patterned gray and silver bark peels in paperlike strips. Sometimes multitrunked.
Catkins/Cones: Insignificant green flowers borne in catkins in spring, to 4 in. (10 cm) long, form scaly seed clusters in late summer, to 2 in. (50 mm) long, persisting to winter.
Plant hardiness: Zones 2–9. Hardy.
Soil: Moist, well-drained. Fertility: Rich–average. 6.0–7.0 pH.
Planting: Full sun. Space 10–15 ft. (3–4.5 m) apart.
Care: Easy. Keep evenly moist. Fertilize annually spring. Prune sparingly in late spring. Propagate by cuttings, layering, seed.
Features: Good choice for accents, borders in cottage, woodland, meadow gardens. Seed attracts birds in winter. Some species are drought tolerant. Leaf miner, borer susceptible.

Tree: Birch, River; Black Birch; Red Birch. *Betula nigra.* BETULACEAE.
Description: Many cultivars of graceful, fast-growing, upright, open, deciduous trees, to 100 ft. (30 m) tall, with light green, oval or diamond-shaped, toothed leaves, to 3 in. (75 mm) long, with white undersides, turning gold in autumn, and with red, white, flaking, paperlike bark. Heritage River Birch, *B. nigra* 'Heritage', is a popular cultivar with pink-tinted bark.
Catkins/Cones: Willowlike male and female catkins, to 1½ in. (38 mm) long, in autumn, form brown cones on female trees, to 1 in. (25 mm) long, the following summer.
Plant hardiness: Zones 4–7.
Soil: Moist, well-drained, sandy. Fertility: Rich–average. 5.5–6.5 pH.
Planting: Full–filtered sun. Space 20–25 ft. (6–7.5 m) apart.
Care: Easy. Keep moist. Prune in late spring. Propagate by cuttings, layers, seed.
Features: Good choice for margins, moist areas in landscapes and water features. Tolerates occasional drought. Seed attracts birds in winter. Somewhat invasive. Shallow rooted. Aphid, birch leaf miner susceptible.

Tree: Birch, Weeping; European White Birch. *Betula pendula.* BETULACEAE.
Description: Several cultivars of graceful, fast-growing, pyramid-shaped, open, deciduous trees, to 60 ft. (18 m) tall, with green, oval or diamond-shaped, veined, toothed leaves, to 2½ in. (65 mm) long, turning gold in autumn, and with white, flaking bark. Cultivars include 'Fastigata', with upright, columnar form; 'Whitespire', a borer-resistant variety; and Young's weeping birch, 'Youngii', a graceful, pendulous tree. Single and multitrunked cultivars are available.
Catkins/Cones: Willowlike male and female catkins, to 2 in. (50 mm) long, in winter, with brown cones on female trees, to 1 in. (25 mm) long, in autumn.
Plant hardiness: Zones 3–7.
Soil: Moist, well-drained humus. Fertility: Rich–average. 5.5–6.5 pH.
Planting: Full–filtered sun. Space 12–15 ft. (3.7–4.5 m) apart.
Care: Easy. Keep moist. Prune in late spring. Propagate by cuttings, seed.
Features: Good choice for accents, borders, screens in cottage, woodland gardens. Seed attracts birds in winter. Tolerates occasional drought. Shallow rooted. Aphid, birch leaf miner susceptible.

Tree: Boxelder; Ash-Leaved Maple. *Acer negundo* subsp. *negundo.* ACERACEAE.
Description: Several cultivars of very fast-growing, spreading, open, short-lived, deciduous trees, 50–70 ft. (15–21 m) tall, with oval, yellow green, sometimes white- or pink-fringed, 3–5-lobed leaves, to 10 in. (25 cm) wide, turning yellow in autumn.
Blooms/Seed: Many ribbonlike, yellow green flowers, to 1½ in. (38 mm) long, in spring before leaves emerge, with typical maplelike, clustered, winged seed summer–autumn.
Plant hardiness: Zones 3–9.
Soil: Damp, well-drained. Fertility: Rich–average. 6.0–7.5 pH.
Planting: Filtered sun–partial shade. Space 10–15 ft. (3–4.5 m) apart.
Care: Easy. Allow surface soil to dry between waterings until established. Fertilize annually until established. Prune sparingly in autumn. Propagate by cuttings, seed.
Features: Good choice for screens, temporary plantings, windbreaks in cold-winter climates. Drops flowers, seed, leaves, requiring maintenance. Very invasive. Shallow rooted. Pest and disease resistant. Leaf burn susceptible in hot, dry climates.

Tree: Camphor tree. *Cinnamomum camphora.* LAURACEAE.
Description: Slow-growing, upright, spreading, dense, broad-leaved evergreen tree, 50–70 ft. (15–21 m) tall and wide though usually smaller, with paddle-shaped, bronze or pink turning light green, aromatic, pointed leaves, to 5 in. (13 cm) long. Leaves simultaneously drop and are replaced in spring.
Blooms/Fruit: Inconspicuous, very fragrant, yellow flowers in spring, form round, black fruit in summer.
Plant hardiness: Zones 9–11.
Soil: Well-drained, sandy. Fertility: Average. 6.5–7.5 pH.
Planting: Full sun. Space 10–15 ft. (3–4.5 m) apart.
Care: Moderate. Allow surface soil to dry between waterings until established. Prune sparingly. Propagate by cuttings, seed.
Features: Good choice for lawns, edgings in open landscapes. Source of camphor oil. Drops leaves, twigs, flowers, fruit. Shallow rooted; avoid planting near pavement. Salt burn, verticillium wilt susceptible.

Tree: Cedar, True. *Cedrus* species. PINACEAE.

Description: About four species of medium-growing, pyramid-shaped, open, sometimes spreading or drooping, coniferous evergreen trees, 100–150 ft. (30–45 m) tall, with deep blue green or green, stiff, clustered needles, 1–2 in. (25–50 mm) long. Species include Atlas cedar, *C. atlantica;* cedar-of-Lebanon, *C. libani;* Cyprus cedar, *C. brevifolia;* and deodar cedar, *C. deodara.*

Cones/Seed: Male cones are egg-shaped, 3–5 in. (75–125 mm) long; female cones are small and pointed with woody scales and winged seed.

Plant hardiness: Zones 7–10. Best in areas with limited winter snow.

Soil: Damp–dry, well-drained. Fertility: Rich–average. 5.5–6.5 pH.

Planting: Full–filtered sun. Space 10–15 ft. (3–4.5 m) apart.

Care: Easy. Allow surface soil to dry between waterings until established. Prune in spring. Protect from snow in cold-winter climates. Propagate by cuttings, seed.

Features: Good choice for accents, screens, specimen in formal, woodland gardens. Male catkins release staining, allergen-bearing pollen in spring. Smog tolerant. Drought tolerant when established. Pest, disease resistant.

Tree: Chaste Tree; Hemp Tree; Wild Pepper. *Vitex agnus-castus.* VERBENEACEAE.

Description: Several cultivars of fast- to medium-growing, broad, spreading, deciduous, frequently multitrunked, shrubby trees, 20–25 ft. (6–7.5 m) tall and wide, with deep green, aromatic, lobed leaves, to 4 in. (10 cm) long, as 5–7 leaflets radiating in a fan with gray undersides.

Blooms/Fruit: Many fragrant, spikelike, pink, purple, red, clustered flowers, to 1 ft. (30 cm) long, in summer, form small, berrylike fruit in autumn.

Plant hardiness: Zones 6–11, depending on cultivar.

Soil: Damp, well-drained. Fertility: Rich–average. 6.5–7.5 pH.

Planting: Full sun. Space 5 ft. (1.5 m) apart, zones 6–8; 8–12 ft. (2.5–3.7 m) apart, zones 9–11.

Care: Easy. Allow surface soil to dry between waterings until established. Prune severely to shrublike form in zones 6–8, moderately in zones 9–11. Mulch in cold-winter climates. Propagate by cuttings, seed.

Features: Good choice for accents, borders, containers, walls in arid climates, small-space gardens. Best in hot-summer climates. Drought tolerant when established. Pest, disease resistant.

Tree: Cherry, Flowering. *Prunus* species and hybrids. ROSACEAE.

Description: About five species and hundreds of hybrids of medium-growing, upright, spreading, short-lived, deciduous ornamental trees, 25–35 ft. (7.5–10.5 m) tall and wide, with smooth, green, veined leaves, to 5 in. (13 cm) long, turning yellow in autumn.

Blooms/Fruit: Many showy, crepelike, pink, rose, white, clustered flowers, 1–2 in. (25–50 mm) wide, in spring, form cherries in late spring or are fruitless.

Plant hardiness: Zones 4–9, depending on cultivar. Best with winter chill.

Soil: Damp, well-drained. Fertility: Rich. 6.5–7.5 pH.

Planting: Full–filtered sun. Space 15–20 ft. (4.5–6 m) apart.

Care: Moderate. Allow surface soil to dry between waterings until established. Fertilize annually in spring until established. Prune after flowering; remove root suckers on grafted stock. Propagate by cuttings, grafting, seed.

Features: Good choice for accents, containers, paths in Asian gardens. Best in cool, low-humidity climates. Smog, pest, fungal disease susceptible.

Tree: Crabapple, Flowering; Showy Crabapple. *Malus floribunda.* ROSACEAE.
Description: Many hybrids of slow-growing, spreading, dense, deciduous trees, to 25 ft. (7.5 m) tall, with fuzzy, deep green to purple, oval, pointed, toothed leaves, 2–3 in. (50–75 mm) long, turning red or brown in autumn.
Blooms/Fruit: Profuse, fragrant, carmine to pink or white flowers in spring, to 1¼ in. (30 mm) wide, in dangling clusters, form yellow or orange, round fruit, to 5/16 in. (8 mm) wide, summer–autumn.
Plant hardiness: Zones 5–9.
Soil: Damp, well-drained. Fertility: Average. 6.5–7.5 pH.
Planting: Full sun. Space 15 ft. (4.5 m) apart.
Care: Easy. Allow surface soil to dry between waterings until established. Fertilize quarterly spring–autumn. Prune in autumn. Protect from sun in hot climates. Propagate by budding, seed.
Features: Good choice for accents, backgrounds, containers, fences, screens in cottage gardens. Fruit attracts birds in winter. Blight, mildew, rust, scab susceptible. Choose disease-resistant hybrids.

Tree: Crape Myrtle. *Lagerstroemia indica.* LYTHRACEAE.
Description: Many cultivars of medium- to slow-growing, sprawling, branching, dense, deciduous shrubby trees, to 20 ft. (6 m) tall and wide, and often with multiple trunks, with shiny, bronze turning deep green, oval, pointed leaves, to 3 in. (75 mm) long, turning orange, red in autumn, and with flaking, gray, brown bark. Genetic dwarf, bush, and standard forms available.
Blooms/Fruit: Many showy, fragrant, red, rose, pink, purple, white, ruffled flowers, to 1½ in. (38 mm) wide, in spring, borne in spikelike, pyramid-shaped clusters, 6–12 in. (15–30 cm) long, form round, brown fruit, to ⅓ in. (8 mm) wide, on woody stems in grapelike clusters that dry and persist through winter.
Plant hardiness: Zones 7–10. Best in mild-winter climates.
Soil: Damp, well-drained. Fertility: Average. 6.5–7.5 pH.
Planting: Full sun. Space 5–30 ft. (1.5–9 m) apart, depending on cultivar.
Care: Easy. Allow surface soil to dry between waterings until established. Fertilize sparingly. Prune in winter. Propagate by cuttings, seed.
Features: Good choice for accents, containers, paths, in coastal, cottage, small-space gardens. Deer resistant. Powdery mildew susceptible.

Tree: Cypress, Bald; Pond Cypress. *Taxodium distichum.* TAXODIACEAE.
Description: Medium-growing, upright, pyramid-shaped, open, coniferous deciduous tree, 100–150 ft. (30–45 m) tall, with green, stiff, oval or flattened needles, to ½ in. (12 mm) long, in fingerlike sprays, turning bronze in autumn, and fibrous, red brown bark. Root projections, or "knees," buttress the trunk, protruding from the water in swampy sites. Growth slows in cold-winter climates.
Cones/Seed: Cones are egg-shaped and knobby, 1 in. (25 mm) wide, in autumn, bearing tiny, flattened seed.
Plant hardiness: Zones 5–11.
Soil: Wet–damp, well-drained. Fertility: Rich–average. 5.0–7.0 pH.
Planting: Full sun. Space 15–20 ft. (4.5–6 m) apart.
Care: Easy. Keep damp. Fertilize annually in spring until established. Prune sparingly. Propagate by cuttings, seed.
Features: Good choice for accents, aquatic plantings, margins in water features, woodland gardens. Pest and disease resistant. Iron chlorosis susceptible.

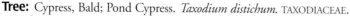

Tree: Cypress, False. *Chamaecyparis* species. CUPRESSACEAE.
Description: Eight species of slow-growing, upright, pyramid-shaped, dense, coniferous evergreen trees, 20–100 ft. (6–45 m) tall, depending on species, with blue, green, yellow, variegated, needle- or scalelike foliage, in spreading sprays, and matted, red brown bark. Cultivated species include Nootka cypress, *C. nootkatensis;* Port Orford cedar, *C. lawsoniana;* and white cedar, *C. thyoides.*
Cones/Seed: Male cones are pink, red, yellow, egg-shaped, ¾ in. (19 mm) long; female cones are woody, ⅜ in. (10 mm) long, with scales and winged seed.
Plant hardiness: Zones 5–9, depending on species.
Soil: Damp, well-drained. Fertility: Average. 5.5–6.5 pH.
Planting: Full sun. Space 10–20 ft. (3–6 m) apart, depending on species.
Care: Easy. Allow surface soil to dry between waterings until established. Fertilize annually in spring until established. Protect from wind. Propagate by seed.
Features: Good choice for accents, allées, containers, hedges, screens in lawns, woodland gardens. Drops leaves, requiring maintenance. Spider mite susceptible.

Tree: Dogwood, Flowering. *Cornus florida.* CORNACEAE.
Description: Many cultivars of fast-growing, spreading, deciduous trees, to 40 ft. (12 m) tall, with shiny, bronze to green, oval leaves, to 6 in. (15 cm) long, turning deep red, purple in autumn. Cultivars include 'Cherokee Chief' and 'Rubra', with pink, red blooms; 'Cherokee Princess' and 'Cloud Nine', with white blooms; 'Pendula', with nodding branches; and 'Welchii', or tricolor dogwood, with variegated red and yellow leaves.
Blooms/Fruit: Profuse, white or pink, flowerlike, 4-petal bracts, 3–4 in. (75–100 mm) wide, in spring, form small, scarlet, berrylike fruit in autumn.
Plant hardiness: Zones 5–10.
Soil: Moist, well-drained. Fertility: Rich. 6.5 pH.
Planting: Full sun–partial shade. Space 20–35 ft. (6–10 m) apart.
Care: Easy. Keep evenly moist. Fertilize in spring. Prune in autumn. Protect from heat in hot climates. Propagate by budding, cuttings.
Features: Good choice for accents, backgrounds in cottage, woodland gardens. Fruit attracts birds. Anthracnose, borer, smog susceptible.

Tree: Elm, Lacebark; Chinese Elm. *Ulmus parvifolia.* ULMACEAE.
Description: Several cultivars of fast-growing, upright and spreading, deciduous or semi-evergreen trees, to 60 ft. (18.3 m) tall and wide, with nodding, willowlike branchlets and deep green, oval, pointed, finely toothed leaves, to 3 in. (75 mm) long, turning bronze, yellow in autumn, and with sycamore-like, flaking, reddish to gray bark.
Blooms/Seed: Inconspicuous, clustered flowers in early spring form numerous winged seed, to 5⁄16 in. (8 mm) wide, in late spring.
Plant hardiness: Zones 5–10.
Soil: Moist–damp, well-drained. Fertility: Average. 5.5–7.0 pH.
Planting: Full sun. Space 15–20 ft. (4.5–6 m) apart.
Care: Moderate. Allow surface soil to dry between waterings until established. Fertilize annually in spring until established. Prune to thin after bloom. Propagate by cuttings, layering, seed.
Features: Good choice for allées, containers, shade in bonsai, patio, roadside plantings. Drops flowers, seeds, leaves, requiring maintenance. Somewhat resistant to Dutch elm disease, elm leaf beetle. Aphid, fire blight, leafhopper, and scale susceptible.

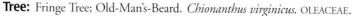

Tree: Fir, White. *Abies concolor.* PINACEAE.

Description: Many cultivars of medium- to slow-growing, upright, pyramid-shaped, coniferous evergreen trees, to 100 ft. (30 m) tall or more, with whorled branches and shiny, blue green or green, flat needles, to 2 in. (50 mm) long, and silver, banded bark with pitch-filled blisters.

Cones/Seed: Female cones are erect, green, brown, purple, cylinder-shaped, to 5 in. (13 cm) long, with woody scales bearing pairs of winged seed.

Plant hardiness: Zones 4–9.

Soil: Damp, well-drained. Fertility: Rich–average. 5.5–7.0 pH.

Planting: Full sun. Space 12–15 ft. (3.7–4.5 m) apart.

Care: Easy. Allow surface soil to dry between waterings until established. Avoid fertilizing and pruning. Propagate by seed.

Features: Good choice for accents, groups, screens in bonsai, woodland gardens and landscape slopes. Seed attracts birds in autumn. Aphid, spider mite susceptible.

Tree: Fringe Tree; Old-Man's-Beard. *Chionanthus virginicus.* OLEACEAE.

Description: Several cultivars of slow-growing, wide and spreading, dense, branching, deciduous shrubby trees, to 30 ft. (9 m) tall and wide, with textured, deep green, lance-shaped, broad, folded, pointed leaves, to 8 in. (20 cm) long, turning yellow in autumn, and with brown, tan bark. Late leafing in spring. Chinese fringe tree, *C. retusus,* a related species, requires similar care.

Blooms/Fruit: Many feathery, cream, white flowers in early summer, to 1 in. (25 mm) wide, in dangling, lacy clusters, to 8 in. (20 cm) long, form oval, blue, purple, mealy fruit in autumn, to ⅝ in. (16 mm) long, in clusters.

Plant hardiness: Zones 4–9. Best with winter chill.

Soil: Damp, well-drained. Fertility: Rich–average. 6.0–7.0 pH.

Planting: Full sun. Space 15–20 ft. (4.5–6 m) apart.

Care: Easy. Allow surface soil to dry between waterings until established. Fertilize annually in spring until established. Avoid pruning. Propagate by cuttings, grafting, layering, seed.

Features: Good choice for accents, backgrounds, containers, edgings, paths, walls in cottage, small-space gardens. Fruit attracts birds. Drops staining fruit. Smog tolerant. Disease resistant. Scale susceptible.

Tree: Ginkgo Tree; Maidenhair Tree. *Ginkgo biloba.* GINKGOACEAE.

Description: Several cultivars of slow-growing, pyramid-shaped to round-crowned, resinous, deciduous trees, rarely to 120 ft. (37 m) tall but usually 30–50 ft. (9–15 m), with fanlike, light green, leathery, fringed leaves, 2–3 in. (50–75 mm) long, turning gold and dropping together in autumn.

Warning

Contact with fruit of ginkgo trees can cause eye irritation or skin rashes in susceptible individuals.

Blooms/Fruit: Inconspicuous flowers on female trees form round, kernel-pitted fruit, to 2 in. (50 mm) wide, with a foul scent remniscent of rancid butter. Choose fruitless male cultivars.

Plant hardiness: Zones 4–9.

Soil: Moist, well-drained. Fertility: Rich. 6.0–7.0 pH.

Planting: Full sun. Space 15–20 ft. (4.5–6 m) apart.

Care: Easy. Keep evenly moist. Fertilize annually in spring until established. Prune sparingly in autumn. Propagate by cuttings, grafting, layering, seed.

Features: Good choice for accents, containers, groups, paths in Asian, small-space gardens and lawns. Pest, disease resistant. Some cultivars smog susceptible.

Tree: Golden-Chain Tree. *Laburnum* × *watereri*. FABACEAE (LEGUMINOSAE).
Description: Several hybrid cultivars of graceful, medium-growing, upright, open, shrubby trees, to 30 ft. (9 m) tall, with cloverlike, green, lobed leaves forming flat, 3-leaflet groups, to 4 in. (10 cm) long, and with green bark.

Warning

All parts and sap of golden-chain trees are hazardous if ingested. Avoid planting in gardens frequented by children or pets.

Blooms/Fruit: Showy yellow flowers borne in wisteria-like, dangling clusters, to 20 in. (50 cm) long, in late spring, form flat, brown, bean-pod-like fruit in autumn.
Plant hardiness: Zones 5–10.
Soil: Damp, well-drained. Fertility: Average–low. 6.5–7.5 pH.
Planting: Filtered sun. Space 6–10 ft. (1.8–3 m) apart.
Care: Easy. Allow surface soil to dry between waterings until established. Fertilize annually in spring until established. Prune in autumn to remove suckers and low branches, maintaining treelike form. Strip seedpods to maintain vigor. Protect from wind. Propagate by budding, grafting, layering, seed.
Features: Good choice for accents in arid, formal, small-space gardens and lawns. Fire blight susceptible.

Tree: Golden Larch. *Pseudolarix ambabilis (P. kaempferi).* PINACEAE.
Description: Single species of medium-growing, upright, pyramid-shaped, branching and layered, coniferous deciduous trees closely related to true larch, usually 20–50 ft. (6–15 m) tall and wide, with smooth, feathery, blue green needles, to 2½ in. (65 mm) long, borne singly or in whorled clusters along the branchlets, turning gold and dropping in autumn.

Blooms/Seed: Cones are clustered and dangling, green turning brown, and rose-shaped, to 3 in. (75 mm) long, with woody scales and 2-winged seed.
Plant hardiness: Zones 6–7. Best with winter chill.
Soil: Moist, well-drained. Fertility: Average. 5.5–7.0 pH.
Planting: Full sun. Space 12–25 ft. (3.7–7.5 m) apart. Avoid crowding to prevent disease.
Care: Moderate. Keep evenly moist. Fertilize annually until established. Prune sparingly in winter. Propagate by seed.
Features: Good choice for accents, backgrounds, foliage color, screens in open landscapes and lawns. Good for seasonal shade. Drops foliage, cones, requiring maintenance. Pest, disease resistant.

Tree: Golden-Rain Tree. *Koelreuteria paniculata.* SAPINDACEAE.
Description: Several cultivars of medium-growing, upright, round-crowned trees, to 45 ft. (13.7 m) tall and wide, with red turning green, divided leaves, to 16 in. (40 cm) long, forming offset rows of toothed or lobed leaflets, turning yellow in autumn.

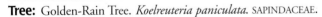

Blooms/Fruit: Showy yellow flowers borne in spiked clusters, to 1 ft. (30 cm) long, in summer, form many red turning brown, 3-sided, parchmentlike fruit containing black seed.
Plant hardiness: Zones 5–9.
Soil: Damp, well-drained. Fertility: Average. 6.5–7.5 pH.
Planting: Full sun. Space 15–20 ft. (4.5–6 m) apart.
Care: Easy. Allow surface soil to dry between waterings until established. Prune to shape after flowering. Propagate by cuttings, seed.
Features: Good choice for accents, backgrounds, edgings, paths, walls in arid, small-space gardens and lawns. Drought tolerant when established. Pest, disease resistant.

Tree: Gum, Australian; Eucalypt; Ironbark. *Eucalyptus* species. MYRTACEAE.
Description: About 700 species of fast-growing, often aromatic, usually upright and spreading, sometimes shrublike, brittle, broad-leaved evergreen trees, varying in height depending on the species, with juvenile leaves of varied shapes and blue green or green, leathery, round, oval, or dagger-shaped mature leaves and papery, persistent or deciduous bark. The genus is divided into the bloodwoods, boxes, gums, peppermints, stringybarks, and ironbarks.
Blooms/Fruit: Distinctive green, pink, red, white, yellow, feathery and plumelike flowers in a woody bud cap, 1–4 in. (25–100 mm) long, form fragrant, blue green, leathery, oily, caplike fruit with many seed.
Plant hardiness: Zones 7–10
Soil: Damp, well-drained, sandy. Fertility: Average. 6.5–7.5 pH.
Planting: Full sun. Space as recommended for species.
Care: Easy–moderate. Keep damp until established. Generally drought tolerant. Prune to shape and remove dead branches. Propagate by cuttings, seed.
Features: Good choice for accents, screens, windbreaks, walls in landscapes. Pest, disease resistant. Eucalyptus longhorn beetle, chlorosis susceptible in alkaline soils.

Tree: Hackberry; Nettle Tree; Sugarberry. *Celtis* species. ULMACEAE.
Description: About 70 species of fast- to medium-growing, upright, round-crowned, deciduous trees, 70–120 ft. (21–37 m) tall, with textured, elmlike, green, droplet-shaped, sharp-toothed, pointed leaves, 3–6 in. (75–150 mm) long, turning yellow in autumn, and with corklike, textured, cinnamon-colored bark.
Blooms/Fruit: Inconspicuous flowers form many edible, round, orange, red, purple fruit, to ¼ in. (6 mm) wide, in summer.
Plant hardiness: Zones 6–8. (*C. occidentalis,* zones 3–8.) Best with winter chill.
Soil: Moist–dry, sandy–clayey. Fertility: Average–low. 6.0–8.0 pH.
Planting: Full sun. Space large species 15–20 ft. (4.5–6 m) apart, small species and dwarf cultivars 10 ft. (3 m) apart.
Care: Easy. Keep damp until established. Avoid fertilizing and pruning. Stake until established. Propagate by cuttings, grafting, layering, seed.
Features: Good choice for allées, edgings, screens in open, natural, prairie gardens and roadside plantings. Good for seasonal shade. Fruit attracts birds. Drought and wind tolerant. Very deep rooted. Harmless leaf gall, or PSYLLIDAE, may disfigure foliage.

Tree: Hawthorn. *Craetagus* species. ROSACEAE.
Description: Many species and hybrid cultivars of medium-growing, spreading, thorny, deciduous shrubby trees, 15–35 ft. (4.5–11 m) tall and wide and often with multiple trunks, with shiny, deep green, lobed or toothed leaves, 2–4 in. (50–100 mm) long, turning red, yellow in autumn.
Blooms/Fruit: Many cream, white, flat flower clusters, to ½ in. (12 mm) wide, in spring, form abundant, edible, shiny, red fruit, to ⅓ in. (8 mm) wide, in summer in showy clusters that persist into winter.
Plant hardiness: Zones 4–9.
Soil: Damp, well-drained. Fertility: Average–low. 6.0–7.0 pH.
Planting: Full–filtered sun. Space 10–12 ft. (3–3.7 m) apart.
Care: Moderate. Keep damp until established. Avoid fertilizing. Prune in autumn to remove suckers, twiggy growth. Propagate by grafting, seed.
Features: Good choice for accents, borders, hedges in natural, wildlife gardens. Fruit attracts birds. Aphid, scale and fireblight susceptible.

Tree: Hemlock, Canadian; Weeping Hemlock. *Tsuga canadensis*. PINACEAE.
Description: Many cultivars of medium-growing, upright, pyramid-shaped, dense, coniferous evergreen trees, to 80 ft. (25 m) tall and often with multiple trunks, with shiny, flat, dark green needles with white undersides, to ¾ in. (19 mm) long, on graceful, nodding branchlets.
Cones/Seed: Female cones are tan and oblong, ¾ in. (19 mm) long, with woody scales and winged seed.
Plant hardiness: Zones 4–9. Best with cool, humid summers, winter chill.
Soil: Moist, well-drained. Fertility: Rich–average. 5.5–6.5 pH.
Planting: Full–filtered sun. Space 10–15 ft. (3–4.5 m) apart as specimens, 5–7 ft. (1.5–2.1 m) as sheared and hedge plantings.
Care: Easy. Keep evenly moist. Drought susceptible. Protect from sun, wind in hot climates. Fertilize annually until established. Prune new growth in spring to shape, shear. Propagate by seed.
Features: Good choice for accents, backgrounds, hedges, screens in landscapes, lawns. Shallow rooted. Salt susceptible. Hemlock woolly aphid susceptible.

Tree: Holly, American. *Ilex opaca*. AQUIFOLIACEAE.
Description: Over 1,000 cultivars of slow-growing, upright, pyramid-shaped to round-crowned, broad-leaved evergreen trees, to 50 ft. (15 m) tall, with shiny or leathery, dark green, oval, pointed, mostly spine-toothed leaves, to 4 in. (10 cm) long.
Blooms/Berries: Insignificant white flowers in spring form round, red or yellow berries, to ⅓ in. (8 mm) wide, in winter, in clusters on female trees. Requires both male and female trees to bear fruit.
Plant hardiness: Zones 6–9.
Soil: Moist, well-drained. Fertility: Rich. 6.0–6.5 pH.
Planting: Full sun–partial shade. Space 10 ft. (3 m) apart. Add acidic compost or leaf mold.
Care: Easy. Allow surface soil to dry between waterings until established. Fertilize spring and autumn. Mulch. Prune sparingly in early spring. Protect from wind. Propagate by cuttings, grafting.
Features: Good choice for backgrounds, barriers, specimens in cottage gardens. Good for cutting. Berries attract birds. Holly bud moth, leaf miner, mealybug, scale susceptible.

Tree: Hornbeam, American; Blue Beech. *Carpinus caroliniana*. BETULACEAE.
Description: A few cultivars of medium- to slow-growing, upright, round-crowned, open, deciduous trees, to 40 ft. (12 m) tall, often with multiple trunks, with deep green, veined, oval, pointed, sharp-toothed leaves, to 4 in. (10 cm) long, turning deep red in autumn, and with smooth, gray bark. European hornbeam, *C. betulus*, a close relative, has a pyramidal form and similar care needs.
Catkins/Nuts: Willowlike catkins, to 4 in. (10 cm) long, in spring, form brown, 3-lobed nuts with leafy bracts, in clusters to 5 in. (13 cm) long, in summer.
Plant hardiness: Zones 3–9. Choose *C. caroliniana* var. *virginiana*, zones 3–5.
Soil: Moist, well-drained. Fertility: Average. 6.0–7.0 pH.
Planting: Full sun–full shade. Space 15–20 ft. (4.5–6 m) apart.
Care: Easy. Keep moist. Fertilize and prune sparingly. Protect from sun, wind in hot climates. Propagate by grafting, seed.
Features: Good choice for accents, paths, screens in landscapes, lawns, roadside plantings. Good for seasonal shade. Disease resistant. Scale susceptible.

Tree: Horse Chestnut; Buckeye. *Aesculus* species. HIPPOCASTANACEAE.

Description: About 13 species of medium-growing, upright, round-crowned, deciduous shrubs or trees, 15–100 ft. (4.5–30 m) tall depending on species, with light to deep green, textured, pointed, toothed leaves, divided into 5- or 7-lobed fanlike leaflets, 8–12 in. (20–30 cm) long, on long leaf stalks.

Blooms/Fruit: Abundant, fragrant, pink, red, white, yellow, spikelike flowers, to 14 in. (35 cm) long, in spring, form ball-like, leathery fruit, to 3 in. (75 mm) wide, enclosing smooth seed and persisting into winter.

Plant hardiness: Zones 3–9, depending on species.

Soil: Damp, well-drained. Fertility: Rich–average. 6.5–7.5 pH.

Planting: Full sun. Space as recommended for species.

Care: Easy–moderate. Allow surface soil to dry between waterings until established. Fertilize and prune sparingly. Protect from sun in hot climates. Propagate by budding, grafting, layering, seed.

Features: Good choice for accents, shade in open landscapes, lawn. Flowers attract hummingbirds. Drops flowers, fruit, leaves, requiring maintenance. Shallow rooted. Invasive. Spider mite susceptible.

> **Warning**
>
> Seed of horse chestnut trees causes severe digestive upset if ingested.

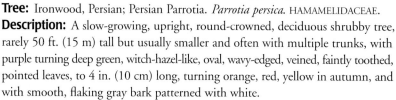

Tree: Ironwood, Persian; Persian Parrotia. *Parrotia persica.* HAMAMELIDACEAE.

Description: A slow-growing, upright, round-crowned, deciduous shrubby tree, rarely 50 ft. (15 m) tall but usually smaller and often with multiple trunks, with purple turning deep green, witch-hazel-like, oval, wavy-edged, veined, faintly toothed, pointed leaves, to 4 in. (10 cm) long, turning orange, red, yellow in autumn, and with smooth, flaking gray bark patterned with white.

Blooms/Fruit: Inconspicuous brown and red flowers in early spring before leaves emerge, form tiny, caplike, seedy fruit in summer.

Plant hardiness: Zones 5–8. Best with winter chill.

Soil: Damp, well-drained. Fertility: Rich–average. 5.5–7.0 pH.

Planting: Full–filtered sun. Space 10–15 ft. (3–4.5 m) apart.

Care: Easy. Allow surface soil to dry between waterings until established. Fertilize annually until established. Prune sparingly. Propagate by cuttings, layers, seed.

Features: Good choice for accents, borders, containers, paths in open and mixed shrub gardens. Deep rooted. Pest and disease resistant.

Tree: Katsura Tree. *Cercidiphyllum japonicum.* CERCIDIPHYLLACEAE.

Description: Several cultivars of graceful, medium- to slow-growing, upright and branching, becoming open and layered, deciduous trees, usually to 50 ft. (15 m) tall and with multiple trunks, with shiny, bronze purple turning blue green, round or heart-shaped, veined, pointed, finely toothed leaves, to 4 in. (10 cm) long, turning yellow in autumn. Popular cultivar is 'Pendulua', with drooping branches.

Blooms/Seed: Many brushlike, red flowers, to ¾ in. (19 mm) long, in early spring before leaves emerge, form beanlike pods containing many seed.

Plant hardiness: Zones 4–8. Best with winter chill.

Soil: Moist, well-drained. Fertility: Rich–average. 6.5–7.0 pH.

Planting: Full–filtered sun. Space 20–30 ft. (6–9 m) apart.

Care: Easy. Keep evenly moist; reduce watering in late summer. Fertilize until established. Prune sparingly. Protect from sun, wind in hot climates. Propagate by cuttings, layering, seed.

Features: Good choice for accents, containers in Asian, small-space gardens and landscapes. Good for seasonal foliage color and shade. Pest, disease resistant.

Tree: Larch. *Larix* species. PINACEAE.

Description: About 10 species of fast- to medium-growing, upright, pyramid-shaped, spreading, coniferous deciduous trees, usually 30–60 ft. (9–18 m) tall, with smooth, often soft, green turning blue green needles, to 1½ in. (38 mm) long, borne singly or in whorled clusters along the branchlets, turning gold and dropping in autumn. Dwarf, pendulous cultivars available.

Cones/Seed: Cones are green turning brown, open, and round, to 1½ in. (38 mm) long, with woody scales and 2-winged seed. Cones prominent winter.

Plant hardiness: Zones 1–7, depending on species. All species are hardy to zone 5. Best with winter chill.

Soil: Moist, well-drained. Fertility: Average. 5.5–7.0 pH.

Planting: Full sun. Space 20–30 ft. (6–9 m) apart. Avoid crowding to prevent spreading fungal disease between trees.

Care: Moderate. Keep evenly moist; *L. laricina* tolerates boggy soil. Fertilize annually until established. Prune sparingly in winter. Propagate by seed.

Features: Good choice for accents, backgrounds, screens in open landscapes and lawns. Good for seasonal foliage color and shade. Larch casebearer and larch branch canker, rust susceptible.

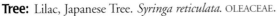

Tree: Lilac, Japanese Tree. *Syringa reticulata.* OLEACEAE.

Description: Several cultivars and varieties of medium-growing, pyramid-shaped, dense, deciduous trees, to 30 ft. (9 m) tall, with shiny, dark green, smooth, oval leaves, to 5 in. (13 cm) long, and with smooth, reddish bark.

Blooms/Berries: Fragrant, tiny, cream, lavender flowers in spring, forming large showy dangling clusters, to 1 ft. (30 cm) long. First blooms 2–3 years after planting. Requires chilling to bloom.

Plant hardiness: Zones 4–8.

Soil: Moist, well-drained. Fertility: Rich. 7.0–7.5 pH.

Planting: Full sun–partial shade. Space 10–15 ft. (3–4.5 m) apart.

Care: Moderate. Keep evenly moist. Fertilize annually in spring until established. Deadhead. Prune sparingly after bloom. Propagate by cuttings, layering.

Features: Good choice for accents, borders in cottage, woodland gardens. Good for cutting. Attracts butterflies. Invasive. Deer resistant. Powdery mildew susceptible.

Tree: Linden. *Tilia* species. TILACEAE.

Description: About 30 species of medium-growing, upright, pyramid-shaped or round-crowned, dense, deciduous trees, usually to 60 ft. (18 m) tall, with shiny, deep green, heart-shaped, pointed, toothed leaves, 4–6 in. (10–15 cm) long, turning yellow in autumn. Species include American linden, *T. americana;* silver linden, *T. tomentosa;* and white linden, *T. heterophylla.*

Blooms/Fruit: Many fragrant, yellow, white, tufted flowers, borne in clusters, to 2 in. (50 mm) wide, in early summer, form round, nutlike fruit cloaked in a papery bract in autumn.

Plant hardiness: Zones 3–9; *T. tomentosa*, zones 5–9.

Soil: Moist, well-drained. Fertility: Rich–average. 6.0–7.0 pH.

Planting: Full–filtered sun. Space 8–12 ft. (2.5–3.7 m) apart.

Care: Easy–moderate. Allow surface soil to dry between waterings until established. Fertilize annually in spring until established. Prune to shape in autumn until mature; prune sparingly thereafter. Propagate by cuttings, layering, seed.

Features: Good choice for accents, allées, backgrounds, screens in landscapes, lawns, and roadside plantings. Aphid, linden borer, Japanese beetle, whitefly and anthracnose susceptible.

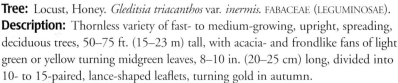

Tree: Locust, Black; False Acacia. *Robinia pseudoacacia.* FABACEAE (LEGUMINOSAE).

Description: Many cultivars of fast- to medium-growing, upright, round-crowned, open, thorny, deciduous trees, to 75 ft. (23 m) tall, with frondlike, green leaves, 8–12 in. (20–30 cm) long, divided into 9-paired oval leaflets, turning yellow in autumn, and with black or deep brown, roughly furrowed bark.

Blooms/Fruit: Depending on the species, many or few, fragrant, pealike, white flowers, borne in dangling clusters, 3–4 in. (75–100 mm) long, in late spring, form reddish brown, podlike fruit, to 4 in. (10 cm) long, containing a row of seed and persisting into winter.

Plant hardiness: Zones 3–10. Best with some winter chill.

Soil: Damp–dry, well-drained. Fertility: Average–low. 6.0–7.5 pH.

Planting: Full sun. Space 10–20 ft. (3–6 m) apart, depending on species.

Care: Easy. Allow surface soil to dry between waterings until established. Avoid fertilizing. Prune to thin, remove suckers in summer. Propagate by cuttings, division, grafting, seed, suckers.

Features: Good choice for low-fertility soil in arid, open gardens. Drops flowers, pods, requiring maintenance. Shallow rooted. Invasive. Drought tolerant. Salt tolerant. Locust borer, leaf miner, scale susceptible.

Tree: Locust, Honey. *Gleditsia triacanthos* var. *inermis.* FABACEAE (LEGUMINOSAE).

Description: Thornless variety of fast- to medium-growing, upright, spreading, deciduous trees, 50–75 ft. (15–23 m) tall, with acacia- and frondlike fans of light green or yellow turning midgreen leaves, 8–10 in. (20–25 cm) long, divided into 10- to 15-paired, lance-shaped leaflets, turning gold in autumn.

Blooms/Fruit: Choose fruitless male cultivars with insignificant flowers.

Plant hardiness: Zones 3–8.

Soil: Moist, well-drained. Fertility: Average–low. 6.0–8.0 pH

Planting: Full sun. Space 15–20 ft. (4.5–6 m) apart.

Care: Easy. Keep moist until established. Avoid fertilizing. Prune to thin, remove crossing branches. Propagate by budding, seed.

Features: Good choice for accents, backgrounds, edgings, paths in open gardens, landscapes, lawns. Drought tolerant when established. Shallow rooted. Invasive. Honey locust borer, locust pod gall, gypsy moth, mimosa webworm, and nectria canker susceptible.

Tree: Magnolia, Saucer. *Magnolia* × *soulangiana.* MAGNOLIACEAE.

Description: Many cultivars of slow-growing, open, deciduous shrubby trees, to 15 ft. (4.5 m) tall, with dark green, oval leaves, to 5 in. (13 cm) long, turning yellow bronze tinged with rose in autumn.

Blooms/Seed: Fragrant, cup-shaped, white, pink, red flowers, to 6 in. (15 cm) wide, in early spring before leaves emerge, form leathery seed clusters, to 3 in. (75 mm) long, in autumn.

Plant hardiness: Zones 5–9.

Soil: Moist, well-drained. Fertility: Rich. Add acidic compost. 5.5–6.5 pH.

Planting: Filtered sun–partial shade. Space 6–10 ft. (1.8–3 m) apart.

Care: Easy. Allow surface soil to dry between waterings until established. Fertilize monthly in spring. Avoid cultivating. Prune autumn. Train to desired shape while young. Protect buds from frost. Propagate by cuttings, layering, seed.

Features: Good choice for accents, containers, shrub borders in cottage, woodland gardens. Drops flowers, leaves, dry pods, requiring maintenance. Shallow rooted. Smog tolerant. Chlorosis susceptible.

Tree: Magnolia, Southern; Bull Bay. *Magnolia grandiflora.* MAGNOLIACEAE.
Description: Many cultivars of medium-growing, dense, broad-leaved evergreen trees, to 100 ft. (30 m) tall, with succulent, waxy, dark green, oval, pointed leaves, to 8 in. (20 cm) long, with rust tan undersides and smooth, brown, gray bark.
Blooms/Seed: Fragrant, cup-shaped, cream white flowers, to 10 in. (25 cm) wide, in late spring and early summer, sometimes repeating bloom in autumn, and form orange, red, leathery, cone-shaped, segmented seed clusters, to 4 in. (10 cm) long, autumn–winter.
Plant hardiness: Zones 7–11.
Soil: Moist, well-drained. Fertility: Rich. Add acidic compost. 6.0–6.5 pH.
Planting: Full–filtered sun. Space 20–30 ft. (6–9 m) apart.
Care: Moderate. Allow surface soil to dry between waterings until established. Fertilize annually in spring until established. Prune in autumn. Protect from wind. Propagate by cuttings, layering, seed.
Features: Good choice for accents, allées in open gardens, landscapes, lawns. Good for shade. Drops flowers, leaves, dry pods, requiring maintenance. Shallow rooted. Magnolia scale, leaf spot, chlorosis susceptible.

Tree: Maple, Amur; Tatarian Maple. *Acer tataricum* var. *ginnala.* ACERACEAE.
Description: Several varieties and cultivars of medium-growing, round-crowned, dense, deciduous trees, to 30 ft. (9 m) tall and wide, with shiny, green, elongated, toothed, 3-lobed leaves, to 3½ in. (90 mm) long, turning yellow, then scarlet in autumn. Dwarf cultivars available. Other *A. tataricum* species are closely related, with similar care needs.
Blooms/Seed: Many tiny, yellow green flowers in early spring, in dangling clusters, to 2 in. (50 mm) long, form typical red, 2-winged seed in summer.
Plant hardiness: Zones 2–9.
Soil: Moist, well-drained. Fertility: Rich–average. 6.5–7.5 pH.
Planting: Full sun–partial shade. Space 15–20 ft. (4.5–6 m) apart.
Care: Moderate. Keep evenly damp. Fertilize annually in spring until established. Prune sparingly in autumn. Protect from wind, sun. Propagate by cuttings, layering, seed.
Features: Good choice for accents, shrub borders, containers in small-space, woodland gardens and lawns. Pest, disease resistant.

Tree: Maple, Full-Moon; Japanese Maple. *Acer japonicum.* ACERACEAE.
Description: Many cultivars of dainty, slow-growing, spreading, deciduous trees, to 30 ft. (9 m) tall, with smooth, light green, oval to round, toothed, 7- to 13-lobed leaves, to 6 in. (15 cm) long, turning bright red in autumn.
Blooms/Seed: Multiple tiny purple or red flowers in spring, in dangling clusters, form typical reddish brown, 2-winged seed in autumn.
Plant hardiness: Zones 5–9. Best with winter chill.
Soil: Moist, well-drained. Fertility: Rich–average. 6.0–7.0 pH.
Planting: Partial shade. Space 12–15 ft. (3.7–4.5 m) apart.
Care: Moderate. Keep evenly moist until established; water when surface soil dries thereafter. Fertilize in spring and autumn. Prune sparingly in autumn. Protect from sun in hot climates, wind. Propagate by cuttings, layering, seed.
Features: Good choice for accents, containers, shrub borders in formal, Japanese-themed, small-space, woodland gardens. Shallow rooted. Smog tolerant. Pest, disease resistant.

Tree: Maple, Japanese. *Acer palmatum.* ACERACEAE.

Description: Many varieties and cultivars of graceful, slow-growing, open, deciduous shrubby trees, to 50 ft. (15 m) tall, with smooth, light green, red, round or oval, toothed, deeply cut leaves, to 4 in. (10 cm) long, tinged red in spring and turning scarlet or yellow in autumn. Beautiful branching habit.

Blooms/Seed: Many tiny, yellow green, red, purple, variegated flowers in early spring, in dangling clusters, form typical 2-winged seed in autumn.

Plant hardiness: Zones 5–10.

Soil: Moist, well-drained. Fertility: Rich–average. 5.5–7.0 pH.

Planting: Full sun–partial shade. Space according to desired effect.

Care: Moderate. Keep evenly damp. Fertilize in spring and autumn. Mulch. Prune sparingly in autumn. Protect from wind, sun. Propagate by cuttings, layering, seed.

Features: Good choice for accents, shrub borders, containers, walls in cottage, small-space, woodland gardens. Subject to leaf-fringe drying. Chlorosis susceptible.

Tree: Maple, Norway. *Acer platanoides.* ACERACEAE.

Description: Many cultivars of fast- to medium-growing, round-crowned, dense, deciduous trees, to 70–90 ft. (21–27 m) tall, with smooth, deep green, purple, oval to round, toothed, 5-lobed leaves, to 6 in. (15 cm) wide, turning yellow in autumn. Cultivars include 'Cleveland II', with compact form; 'Crimson King' and 'Royal Red', with deep red to purple leaves; and 'Variegatum', with white-fringed leaves.

Blooms/Seed: Multiple tiny yellow green flowers in spring, in dangling clusters, form typical reddish brown, 2-winged seed in autumn.

Plant hardiness: Zones 3–9. Best with winter chill.

Soil: Moist, well-drained. Fertility: Rich–average. 6.0–7.0 pH.

Planting: Partial shade. Space 20–30 ft. (6–9 m) apart.

Care: Moderate. Keep evenly moist until established; water when soil dries thereafter. Fertilize in spring until established. Prune in autumn. Propagate by cuttings, layering, seed.

Features: Good choice for accents, allées, screens, specimens in open, woodland gardens and lawns. Drops flowers, seed, requiring maintenance. Shallow rooted. Invasive. Smog tolerant. Pest, disease resistant. Iron chlorosis susceptible.

Tree: Maple, Paperbark. *Acer griseum.* ACERACEAE.

Description: A few cultivars of slow-growing, upright, columnar or spreading, dense, deciduous trees, to 40 ft. (12 m) tall, with smooth, deep green, oval to round, toothed, 3-lobed leaves, to 3 in. (75 mm) wide, with silvery undersides, turning red in autumn, and with red brown, papery, flaking bark.

Blooms/Seed: Few inconspicuous red flowers in early spring, in dangling clusters, form showy, red, 2-winged seed in summer.

Plant hardiness: Zones 4–9. Best with winter chill.

Soil: Moist, well-drained. Fertility: Rich–average. 6.0–7.0 pH.

Planting: Full–filtered sun. Space 15–20 ft. (4.5–6 m) apart.

Care: Moderate. Keep evenly damp. Fertilize annually in spring until established. Prune sparingly in autumn. Protect from wind, sun. Propagate by grafting, seed.

Features: Good choice for accents, shrub borders in woodland gardens and lawns. Pest, disease resistant.

Tree: Maple, Red; Scarlet Maple; Swamp Maple. *Acer rubrum.* ACERACEAE.
Description: Many cultivars of fast- to medium-growing, upright, round-crowned, dense, deciduous trees, to 120 ft. (37 m) tall, with shiny, deep green, oval to round, deeply toothed, 3- to 5-lobed leaves, to 6 in. (15 cm) wide, with pale green undersides, turning scarlet in autumn, and with red turning brown, smooth bark.
Blooms/Seed: Many showy, red, yellow flowers, in dangling clusters, to 1 in. (25 mm) long, in early spring before leaves emerge, form showy, red, 2-winged seed in late spring.
Plant hardiness: Zones 2–9. Best with winter chill.
Soil: Moist, well-drained. Fertility: Rich–average. 6.0–7.0 pH.
Planting: Full–filtered sun. Space 15–20 ft. (4.5–6 m) apart.
Care: Moderate. Keep evenly damp. Fertilize annually in spring until established. Prune sparingly in autumn. Propagate by cuttings, layering, seed.
Features: Good choice for accents, allées, borders, screens in woodland gardens, lawns, roadside plantings. Shallow rooted. Pest, disease resistant. Smog susceptible.

Tree: Maple, Silver; Soft Maple; White Maple. *Acer saccharinum.* ACERACEAE.
Description: Many cultivars of fast-growing, upright, spreading, open, brittle, deciduous trees, 90–120 ft. (27–37 m) tall, with shiny, deep green, round, deeply toothed, 5-lobed leaves, to 6 in. (15 cm) wide, with silver white undersides, turning orange, red, yellow in autumn, and with silver gray, flaking bark.
Blooms/Seed: Many pinkish green flowers, in dangling clusters, to ½ in. (12 mm) long, in early spring before leaves emerge, form showy, red, 2-winged seed in late spring.
Plant hardiness: Zones 2–9. Best with winter chill.
Soil: Moist, well-drained. Fertility: Rich–average. 5.5–7.0 pH.
Planting: Full–filtered sun. Space 15–20 ft. (4.5–6 m) apart.
Care: Moderate. Keep evenly damp. Fertilize annually in spring until established. Prune sparingly in autumn. Propagate by cuttings, layering, seed.
Features: Good choice for accents, allées, borders, screens in woodland gardens, lawns, roadside plantings. Weak crotched branches are susceptible to breakage. Shallow rooted. Invasive. Aphid, scale and chlorosis, smog susceptible.

Tree: Maple, Trident. *Acer buergeranum.* ACERACEAE.
Description: A few varieties and cultivars of slow-growing, upright, round-crowned, dense, deciduous trees, usually to 25 ft. (7.5 m) tall, with shiny, deep green, oval, shallow- and 3-lobed leaves, to 4 in. (10 cm) wide, with pale green undersides, turning orange, red in autumn, and with greenish brown, flaking bark.
Blooms/Seed: Many, yellow flowers in early spring, in broad, dangling clusters, form yellow green, 2-winged seed in summer.
Plant hardiness: Zones 6–9.
Soil: Moist, well-drained. Fertility: Rich–average. 6.0–7.0 pH.
Planting: Full–filtered sun. Space 15–20 ft. (4.5–6 m) apart.
Care: Moderate. Keep evenly damp. Fertilize annually in spring until established. Stake, brace to train growth. Prune in autumn. Protect from wind, sun. Propagate by cuttings, grafting, seed.
Features: Good choice for accents, shrub borders, shade in Asian, bonsai, patio, small-space, woodland gardens and lawns. Pest, disease resistant.

Tree: Mountain Ash, European; Rowan Tree. *Sorbus aucuparia.* ROSACEAE.
Description: Several cultivars of medium-growing, upright, oval- or round-crowned, dense, deciduous trees, to 60 ft. (18 m) tall, with frondlike, green leaves, 4–10 in. (10–25 cm) long, divided into 13- or 15-paired, blade-shaped, sharp-toothed leaflets, to 2½ in. (65 mm) long, turning red in autumn, and with gray brown bark. Cultivars include 'Asplenifolia' with deeply cut leaves.
Blooms/Fruit: Many showy white flowers, to ¼ in. (6 mm) wide, borne in flat clusters, in spring, form round, orange, red, mealy, berrylike, clustered fruit, to ¼ in. (6 mm) wide, in late summer.
Plant hardiness: Zones 1–9. Best with winter chill and mild summers.
Soil: Moist, well-drained. Fertility: Rich–average. 6.0–7.0 pH.
Planting: Full sun. Space 10–15 ft. apart.
Care: Easy. Allow surface soil to dry between waterings until established. Fertilize annually in spring until established. Prune to shape in autumn. Protect from sun, wind in hot climates. Propagate by budding, layering, seed.
Features: Good choice for accents, containers, espaliers in small-space gardens and landscape beds. Drops staining fruit, requiring maintenance. Canker, fireblight and sawfly, scale susceptible.

Tree: Oak, Pin; Spanish Oak; Swamp Oak. *Quercus palustris.* FAGACEAE.
Description: Several cultivars of medium-growing, upright, pyramid-shaped, open, deciduous trees, to 80 ft. (24 m) tall, with shiny, deep green, lance-shaped, 5- to 7-lobed, pointed, deeply cut leaves, to 5 in. (13 cm) long, turning brown, red, yellow in autumn, persisting into winter, and with gray brown, furrowed bark.
Blooms/Nuts: Many inconspicuous, pale green, willowlike, dangling or spiking catkins in spring, form round acorns, to ¾ in. (19 mm) long, in autumn, with cup-shaped caps partially surrounding each nutshell.
Plant hardiness: Zones 2–10.
Soil: Moist, well-drained. Fertility: Rich. 6.0–7.0 pH.
Planting: Full sun. Space 15–25 ft. (4.5–7.5 m) apart.
Care: Moderate. Keep evenly moist. Fertilize annually in spring until established. Prune in autumn. Propagate by cuttings, grafting, seed.
Features: Good choice for accents, paths, screens in open landscapes and lawns. Drops leaves, acorns, requiring maintenance. Gypsy moth, oak-leaf pruner, scale and anthracnose, canker, chlorosis, gall, oak wilt susceptible.

Tree: Oak, Red; Northern Red Oak. *Quercus rubra (Q. borealis).* FAGACEAE.
Description: Several cultivars of fast-growing, upright, pyramid-shaped turning round-crowned and branching, open, deciduous trees, to 80 ft. (24 m) tall, with shiny, red turning deep green, oval, 7- to 11-lobed, pointed, deeply cut leaves, turning red in autumn, and with deep gray to chocolate, roughly furrowed bark.
Catkins/Nuts: Many inconspicuous, pale green, willowlike, dangling or spiking catkins in spring, form acorns in autumn, to 1 in. (25 mm) long, with cup-shaped caps partially surrounding each nutshell.
Plant hardiness: Zones 2–9. Best with winter chill.
Soil: Moist, well-drained. Fertility: Rich. 5.5–7.0 pH.
Planting: Full sun. Space 15–25 ft. (4.5–7.5 m) apart.
Care: Moderate. Keep moist. Pinch to train, prune in autumn. Transplants easily in spring. Propagate by cuttings, grafting, seed.
Features: Good choice for accents, screens in open landscapes. Drops leaves, acorns, requiring maintenance. Canker, gall, gypsy moth and oak wilt susceptible.

Tree: Oak, Scarlet. *Quercus coccinea.* FAGACEAE.
Description: Several cultivars of medium-growing, upright, pyramid-shaped or round-crowned, open, deciduous trees, to 80 ft. (24 m) tall, with shiny, deep green, lance-shaped, 7- to 9-lobed, pointed, very deeply cut leaves, to 6 in. (15 cm) long, turning red in autumn, persisting into winter, and with gray brown, platelike bark.
Catkins/Nuts: Many inconspicuous, pale green, willowlike, dangling or spiking catkins in spring, form round acorns in autumn, to 1 in. (25 mm) long, with cup-shaped caps half surrounding each nutshell.
Plant hardiness: Zones 4–9. Best with winter chill.
Soil: Moist, well-drained. Fertility: Rich. 5.5–7.0 pH.
Planting: Full sun. Space 15–25 ft. (4.5–7.5 m) apart.
Care: Moderate. Allow surface soil to dry between waterings. Fertilize annually in spring until established. Prune in autumn. Propagate by cuttings, grafting, seed.
Features: Good choice for accents, allées, paths, screens in open landscapes, lawns, and roadside plantings. Drops leaves, acorns, requiring maintenance. Gypsy moth, oak-leaf pruner, scale and anthracnose, canker, gall, chlorosis, oak wilt susceptible.

Tree: Oak, White. *Quercus alba.* FAGACEAE.
Description: Several cultivars of fast-growing, upright, round-crowned and branching, open, deciduous trees, to 100 ft. (30 m) tall, with shiny, pink turning deep green, oval, 5- to 9-lobed, rounded, deeply cut leaves, to 9 in. (23 cm) long, turning purple, red in autumn, and with gray, roughly furrowed bark.
Catkins/Nuts: Many inconspicuous, pale green, willowlike, dangling or spiking catkins in spring, form red, round acorns in autumn, to 1 in. (25 mm) long, with cup-shaped caps partially surrounding each nutshell.
Plant hardiness: Zones 4–8. Best with winter chill.
Soil: Damp, well-drained. Fertility: Rich. 5.5–7.0 pH.
Planting: Full sun. Space 20–25 ft. (6–7.5 m) apart.
Care: Moderate. Allow surface soil to dry between waterings. Fertilize annually in spring. Prune in autumn. Propagate by cuttings, grafting, seed.
Features: Good choice for accents, paths, screens in open landscapes and lawns. Drops twigs, leaves, acorns, requiring maintenance. Gypsy moth, oak-leaf pruner, scale, anthracnose, canker, chlorosis, gall, oak wilt susceptible.

Tree: Pagoda Tree, Japanese. *Sophora japonica.* FABACEAE (LEGUMINOSAE).
Description: Several cultivars of medium-growing, upright, vase-shaped becoming round-crowned, open, deciduous trees, to 80 ft. (24 m) tall, with frondlike green leaves, 7–10 in. (18–25 cm) long, divided into 3- to 8-paired, oval or lance-shaped leaflets, to 2 in. (50 mm) long, with light green undersides, turning yellow in autumn, and with gray green, roughly furrowed bark.
Blooms/Fruit: Many showy, white, yellow, pealike flowers, in summer when mature, to ½ in. (12 mm) long, borne in spiking clusters, to 1 ft. (30 cm) long, form brown, beanlike pods in autumn, to 3 in. (75 mm) long, containing smooth seed.
Plant hardiness: Zones 4–10. Best with summer heat.
Soil: Damp, well-drained. Fertility: Average–low. 6.5–7.5 pH.
Planting: Full sun. Space 15–20 ft. (4.5–6 m) apart.
Care: Moderate. Allow surface soil to dry between waterings. Prune sparingly. Protect from ice. Propagate by cuttings, layering, grafting, seed.
Features: Good choice for accents, containers in small-space gardens. Drops staining flowers, seedpods, requiring maintenance. Smog tolerant. Pest, disease resistant.

Tree: Pear, Callery. *Pyrus calleryana.* ROSACEAE.

Description: Many cultivars of fast-growing, upright, round-crowned or columnar, open, thorny, semi-evergreen trees, to 50 ft. (15 m) tall, with shiny, green, broadly oval, pointed, leaves, to 3 in. (75 mm) long, turning red, yellow in autumn, and with gray green, smooth bark. Avoid brittle, disease-susceptible, short-lived 'Bradford' cultivar; choose instead 'Aristocrat', 'Chanticleer', 'Redspire', or 'Whitehouse'.

Blooms/Fruit: Many showy, white, simple flowers in early spring, to 1 in. (25 mm) wide, in stemmed clusters, form small, brown, pearlike, inedible fruit or are fruitless, depending on cultivar.

Plant hardiness: Zones 5–9. Best with winter chill.

Soil: Damp, well-drained. Fertility: Average. 6.5–7.5 pH.

Planting: Full sun. Space 8–12 ft. (2.5–3.7 m) apart.

Care: Easy. Allow surface soil to dry between waterings until established. Fertilize annually in spring. Prune in autumn. Propagate by budding, grafting.

Features: Good choice for accents, backgrounds, borders, containers, edgings, paths, walls in small-space, formal gardens. Smog tolerant. Fireblight resistant.

Tree: Pepper Tree, California; Australian Pepper. *Schinus molle.* ANACARDIACEAE.

Description: Several cultivars of fast-growing, upright, spreading, deciduous, trees, 20–50 ft. (6–15 m) tall and wide, with smooth, frondlike, light green, aromatic leaves, to 9 in. (23 cm) long, as 15- to 41-paired, lance-shaped leaflets along each nodding branch, and with rough, cinnamon, gnarled, flaking bark.

Blooms/Fruit: Many fragrant, spikelike, dangling, yellow, white, clustered flowers, to 6 in. (15 cm) long, in spring, form small, red, clustered, berrylike, edible fruit in autumn, persisting into winter.

Plant hardiness: Zones 8–11. Best in hot-summer climates.

Soil: Damp, well-drained. Fertility: Average–low. 6.5–7.5 pH.

Planting: Full sun. Space 5 ft. (1.5 m) apart, zones 6–8; 8–12 ft. (2.5–3.7 m) apart, zones 9–11.

Care: Easy. Allow surface soil to dry between waterings until established. Prune in autumn. Propagate by cuttings, seed.

Features: Good choice for accents, walls in arid climates, open gardens, lawns. Drought tolerant when established. Drops twigs, leaves, flowers, fruit, requiring maintenance. Shallow rooted. Invasive. Disease resistant. Black scale susceptible.

Tree: Pine, Eastern White. *Pinus strobus.* PINACEAE.

Description: Many cultivars of fast-growing, conical to rounded, coniferous, evergreen trees, to 120 ft. (36 m) tall, with smooth, blue or gray green, round, slender needles, to 6 in. (15 cm) long, borne in basal, 5-needle clusters.

Catkins/Cones: Male cones, to 3 in. (75 mm) long, resemble feathery catkins; female cones are globular and pointed, to 6 in. (15 cm) long, with woody scales and winged seed.

Plant hardiness: Zones 3–9.

Soil: Damp–dry, well-drained. Fertility: Average–low. 6.0–7.0 pH.

Planting: Full sun. Space 15 ft. (4.5 m) apart.

Care: Easy. Allow surface soil to dry between waterings until established. Avoid fertilizing. Prune to shape in spring, removing half of new growth "candles." Propagate by cuttings, seed.

Features: Good choice for accents, shrub borders, containers, screens in woodland gardens and lawns.

Tree: Pine, Lace-Bark. *Pinus bungeana*. PINACEAE.

Description: Several cultivars of slow-growing, pyramid-shaped becoming round-crowned, brittle, coniferous, evergreen trees, to 75 ft. (23 m) tall, with smooth, deep green, stiff, twisted needles, to 3 in. (75 mm) long, borne in bundled, 3-needle clusters, and with smooth, gray bark becoming flaking, platelike, and white.

Catkins/Cones: Male cones resemble feathery catkins; female cones are yellow brown, egg-shaped, to 3 in. (75 mm) long, with woody scales and winged seed.

Plant hardiness: Zones 4–9.

Soil: Damp–dry, well-drained. Fertility: Average. 6.0–7.0 pH.

Planting: Full sun. Space 15 ft. (4.5 m) apart.

Care: Easy. Allow surface soil to dry between waterings until established. Avoid fertilizing. Prune sparingly in spring, removing a third of new growth "candles." Propagate by cuttings, seed.

Features: Good choice for accents, shrub borders, screens in Asian, formal gardens and lawns.

Tree: Pine, Scots; Scotch Pine. *Pinus sylvestris*. PINACEAE.

Description: Many cultivars of medium-growing, upright, pyramid-shaped becoming irregular, open, coniferous, evergreen trees, 75–100 ft. (23–30 m) tall, with smooth, blue green, stiff, round, contorted needles, to 3 in. (75 mm) long, borne in basal, paired clusters, and with reddish-gray bark.

Catkins/Cones: Male cones resemble feathery catkins, to 3 in. (75 mm) long; female cones are blue to yellow green, oval and pointed, to 2½ in. (65 mm) long, with woody scales and winged seed.

Plant hardiness: Zones 2–9.

Soil: Damp, well-drained. Fertility: Average–low. 6.0–7.0 pH.

Planting: Full sun. Space 15–20 ft. (4.5–6 m) apart.

Care: Easy. Allow surface soil to dry between waterings until established, and deep water during drought. Avoid fertilizing. Prune to shape in spring, removing half of new growth "candles." Propagate by cuttings, seed.

Features: Good choice for accents, screens in woodland gardens. Popular as cut, sheared tree for holiday decorations. Aphid, beetle, European pine shoot moth, scale and rust susceptible.

Tree: Pistache, Chinese; Chinese Pistachio. *Pistacia chinensis*. ANACARDIACEAE.

Description: A few cultivars of medium- to slow-growing, upright, round-crowned, open becoming dense, deciduous trees, to 60 ft. (18 m) tall, with shiny, frondlike, deep green leaves, 1 ft. (30 cm) long, divided into 6- to 10-paired, lance-shaped leaflets, to 2½ in. (65 mm) long, turning orange, red in autumn, and with pinkish gray, flaking bark.

Blooms/Fruit: Insignificant flowers in spring form round, red turning black, leathery, clustered fruit on female trees in summer, to 1½ in. (38 mm) wide, containing seed. Choose fruitless male cultivars.

Plant hardiness: Zones 6–9.

Soil: Damp, well-drained. Fertility: Average. 6.0–7.5 pH.

Planting: Full sun. Space 20–25 ft. (6–7.5 m) apart.

Care: Easy. Allow surface soil to dry between waterings until established. Avoid fertilizing. Stake to support. Prune to head and shape in autumn. Propagate by budding, grafting, seed.

Features: Good choice for accents, allées, backgrounds, containers, fences, screens in landscapes, roadside plantings, and on sloped sites. Pest resistant. Verticillium wilt susceptible.

Tree: Plane Tree, London; Sycamore. *Platanus* × *acerifolia*. PLATANACEAE.

Description: Hybrids and cultivars of fast-growing, upright, round-crowned or branching, open to dense, deciduous trees, to 120 ft. (37 m) tall, with textured, maplelike, green, 3- to 5-lobed, veined, toothed leaves, to 8 in. (20 cm) long and wide, turning brown, yellow in autumn, and with patchy, brown, older bark, flaking to reveal irregular, light gray, younger bark.

Blooms/Seed: Insignificant hairy flowers in spring form dangling, round, brown seed clusters, to 1½ in. (38 mm) wide, in autumn, persisting through winter.

Plant hardiness: Zones 5–9. Best with winter chill.

Soil: Moist–damp, well-drained. Fertility: Rich–average. 6.5–7.5 pH.

Planting: Full sun. Space 20–30 ft. (6–9 m) apart.

Care: Easy. Allow surface soil to dry between waterings until established. Fertilize annually in spring until established. Prune in autumn to shape, pollard. Propagate by cuttings, grafting, layering, seed.

Features: Good choice for accents, allées, backgrounds, canopies, paths, screens, walls in open landscapes, lawns, roadside plantings. Drops twigs, leaves, fruit, requiring maintenance. Oak root fungus resistant. Sycamore lace bug, scale and anthracnose susceptible.

Tree: Poplar; Aspen; Cottonwood. *Populus* species. SALICACEAE.

Description: Nearly 40 species of fast-growing, upright, columnar or branching, open, short-lived, deciduous trees, varying in height depending on the species, with shiny, light green, heart-shaped, pointed, toothed leaves, 2–5 in. (50–125 mm) long, sometimes with light green, silver undersides, turning gold, red, yellow in autumn, and with white, gray green, gray, rough, furrowed bark.

Catkins/Seed: Willowlike catkins, to 2 in. (50 mm) long, in early spring before leaves, form brown, clustered, hairy seed, ½–1 in. (12–25 mm) long, in spring.

Plant hardiness: Zones 2–9, depending on species.

Soil: Moist, well-drained. Fertility: Rich–average. 5.5–7.0 pH.

Planting: Full sun. Space as recommended for species.

Care: Moderate. Keep evenly moist. Avoid fertilizing. Prune in autumn to shape, remove suckers. Propagate by cuttings, grafting, seed, suckers.

Features: Good choice for borders, fences, groups, screens in cold-climate, mountain gardens. Good for temporary plantings. Short-lived. Drops twigs, leaves, seed, requiring maintenance. Shallow rooted. Very invasive. Generally disease resistant. Poplar curculio, cottonwood leaf beetle, scale susceptible.

Tree: Red Cedar. *Juniperus virginiana*. CUPRESSACEAE.

Description: Many cultivars of medium-growing, upright, pyramid-shaped, coniferous evergreen trees, to 75 ft. (23 m) tall, with shiny, blue green or deep green, aromatic needles or scaly, cedarlike foliage with overlapped plates, and with reddish brown, furrowed bark.

Blooms/Cones: Yellow, catkinlike, male cones and light blue, aromatic, pulpy, berrylike female cones appear in spring, ripening in autumn.

Plant hardiness: Zones 3–9.

Soil: Damp, well-drained loam. Fertility: Average. 5.5–7.5 pH.

Planting: Full sun. Space 12–15 ft. (3.7–4.5 m) apart.

Care: Easy. Allow surface soil to dry between waterings. Fertilize annually in spring until established. Propagate by cuttings, grafting, seed.

Features: Good choice for accents, screens in open, woodland gardens, landscapes. Aphid, borer, spider mite and juniper blight susceptible.

Tree: Redbud, Eastern. *Cercis canadensis.* FABACEAE (LEGUMINOSAE).

Description: Several cultivars of fast-growing, spreading, deciduous trees, to 40 ft. (12 m) tall, with glossy, bronze to purple, heart-shaped leaves, to 4 in. (10 cm) long, turning yellow in autumn.

Blooms/Fruit: Many rose pink, purple, white flowers in early spring, ½ in. (13 mm) wide, in clusters, form pealike, clustered fruit, to 3½ in. (90 mm) long, in late spring. First blooms 4–5 years after planting.

Plant hardiness: Zones 5–9.

Soil: Moist, well-drained. Fertility: Rich. 6.5–7.5 pH.

Planting: Open–filtered shade. Space 20 ft. (6 m) apart.

Care: Easy. Allow surface soil to dry between waterings until established. Fertilize semi-monthly spring–autumn. Mulch. Prune in autumn. Protect from sun in hot climates. Propagate by cuttings, layering, seed.

Features: Good choice for backgrounds in cottage, woodland gardens. Best in cold-winter climates. Good companion for dogwood. Disease resistant.

Tree: Redwood, Dawn. *Metasequoia glyptostroboides.* TAXODIACEAE.

Description: Single ancient species of fast-growing, pyramid-shaped, coniferous, deciduous tree, to 100 ft. (30 m) tall, with shiny, flat, deep green needles, ½–1½ in. (12–38 mm) long, with silvery undersides, turning golden red in autumn, with fibrous, red, fissured bark, and with trunks to 9 ft. (2.7 m) wide. Classified first by fossil record, then rediscovered in 1945 in Szechwan, China. Related trees, coast redwood, *Sequoia sempervirens,* and giant sequoia, *Sequoiadendron giganteum,* with great size and similar general appearance, are evergreens.

Blooms/Cones: Stemless, drooping, spikelike male cones and round, green, stemmed, female cones appear in spring, ripening in summer, containing scaly, winged seed.

Plant hardiness: Zones 5–9. Best with winter chill.

Soil: Moist, well-drained. Fertility: Rich–average. 6.0–7.0 pH.

Planting: Full sun. Space 20–30 ft. (6–9 m) apart.

Care: Easy. Keep evenly moist. Fertilize annually. Prune suckers. Protect from salt, sun in hot, coastal climates. Propagate by cuttings, seed, suckers.

Features: Good choice for accents, seasonal screens in open landscapes. Shallow rooted. Pest, disease resistant.

Tree: Sassafras. *Sassafras albidum.* LAURACEAE.

Description: A few cultivars of fast- to medium-growing, upright, irregular, open, deciduous trees, to 60 ft. (18 m) tall, with fragrant bark, often with multiple trunks, and with shiny, green, aromatic, oval or mitten-shaped, broad, often lobed leaves, to 5 in. (13 cm) long and wide, turning gold, red in autumn, and with red brown bark.

Blooms/Fruit: Many fragrant, ribbonlike, yellow flowers, to 2 in. (50 mm) long, in clusters in spring, form deep blue, purple, clustered, berrylike fruit, to ½ in. (12 mm) wide, on red stalks in autumn.

Plant hardiness: Zones 4–9.

Soil: Damp, well-drained. Fertility: Average–poor. 6.0–7.0 pH.

Planting: Full sun. Space 15–20 ft. (4.5–6 m) apart.

Care: Easy. Allow surface soil to dry between waterings. Avoid fertilizing and transplanting. Prune suckers in autumn to maintain treelike appearance. Propagate by cuttings, seed.

Features: Good choice for accents, allées, screens in open landscapes and roadside plantings. Disease resistant. Japanese beetle, sassafras stem borer, gypsy moth susceptible.

Tree: Serviceberry; Juneberry; Shadblow. *Amelanchier* species. ROSACEAE.
Description: About 25 species of medium-growing, upright, round-crowned, open, deciduous shrubby trees, 20–40 ft. (6–12 m) tall, depending on species, often with multiple trunks, and with shiny, deep green, oval, pointed, toothed leaves, to 3 in. (75 mm) long, turning orange, yellow in autumn, and with silver gray, white bark.
Blooms/Fruit: Many ribbonlike, white flowers, to 2 in. (50 mm) long, in clusters in spring as leaves emerge, form edible, deep blue, berrylike fruit, to ⅓ in. (8 mm) wide, in summer.
Plant hardiness: Zones 1–8, depending on species.
Soil: Moist, well-drained. Best with winter chill.
Planting: Full sun. Space 8–15 ft. (2.5–4.5 m) apart.
Care: Moderate. Keep evenly moist. Fertilize annually in spring until established. Prune in autumn; remove suckers to maintain treelike appearance. Propagate by seed, suckers.
Features: Good choice for accents, borders, containers, margins, paths, screens in cottage, small-space, woodland gardens and water features. Fruit attracts birds. Drops flowers, fruit, requiring maintenance. Lacewing, scale, spider mite and fireblight susceptible.

Tree: Silver-Bell Tree; Wild Olive. *Halesia carolina.* STYRACACEAE.
Description: Slow-growing, narrow, dense, deciduous tree, to 40 ft. (12 m) tall and 20 ft. (6 m) wide, with smooth, light green, oval leaves, to 4 in. (10 cm) long, turning yellow in autumn, with black, brown, gray, roughly furrowed bark.
Blooms/Fruit: Abundant, white to pink, bell-shaped, drooping flowers, ¾ in. (18 mm) long, in spring, form winged fruit in autumn.
Plant hardiness: Zones 5–11. Hardy.
Soil: Moist, well-drained soil humus. Fertility: Rich. 5.0–6.5 pH.
Planting: Partial shade. Space 15–20 ft. (4.5–6 m) apart.
Care: Easy. Generally care free. Keep moist. Fertilize annually in spring. Limit pruning. Protect from drying wind. Transplants readily. Propagate by cuttings, layering, seed.
Features: Good choice for spring flower accent and attractive addition near azaleas or rhododendrons. Pest, disease resistant.

Tree: Snowbell, Japanese; Snowdrop; Storax. *Styrax japonicus.* STYRACACEAE.
Description: Several cultivars of medium- to slow-growing, upright, spreading, deciduous shrubby trees, to 30 ft. (9 m) tall, often with multiple trunks, with shiny, deep green, lance-shaped, pointed, veined leaves, to 3 in. (75 mm) long, turning red, yellow in autumn, and with smooth, gray, fissured bark. A related species, fragrant snowbell, *S. obassia*, with fragrant flowers, has similar care needs.
Blooms/Fruit: Many showy, sometimes fragrant, yellow, bell-shaped flowers, to ¾ in. (19 mm) long, in dangling clusters in early summer, to 8 in. (20 cm) long, form mealy, berrylike fruit, to ½ in. (12 mm) long, containing seed, in autumn.
Plant hardiness: Zones 5–9. Protect from cold until established, zones 5–7.
Soil: Moist, well-drained. Fertility: Rich–average. 5.5–7.0 pH.
Planting: Full–filtered sun. Space 15–20 ft. (4.5–6 m apart).
Care: Moderate. Allow surface soil to dry between waterings until established. Fertilize annually in spring until established. Prune to shape after bloom, remove suckers. Avoid transplanting. Propagate by grafting, layering, seed.
Features: Good choice for accents, beds, containers, paths, walls in Asian, formal, small-space gardens and lawns. Pest, disease resistant.

Tree: Sourwood; Sorrel Tree; Titi. *Oxydendrum arboreum.* ERICACEAE.
Description: Single species of medium-growing, upright, pyramid-shaped, deciduous tree, eventually 50–80 ft. (15–24 m) tall but usually less than 30 ft. (9 m), with shiny, bronze turning deep green, lance-shaped, pointed, finely toothed leaves, to 8 in. (20 cm) long, turning orange, purple, red, yellow in autumn, and with brown gray bark.
Blooms/Fruit: Many fragrant, lily-of-the-valley–like, creamy white, bell-shaped flowers, to 5⁄16 in. (8 mm) long, in dangling clusters, in summer, form leathery green fruit caps containing seed, in branched, spreading clusters, in autumn.
Plant hardiness: Zones 5–9. Best with winter chill, temperate summers.
Soil: Moist, well-drained. Fertility: Rich. 5.5–6.5 pH.
Planting: Full sun–partial shade. Space 8–12 ft. (2.4–3.7 m) apart.
Care: Easy. Allow surface soil to dry between waterings until established. Avoid cultivating beneath tree. Prune in autumn. Propagate by seed.
Features: Good choice for accents, beds, borders, containers, edgings in formal, small-space gardens and patios. Good for seasonal shade. Attracts bees. Pest, disease resistant.

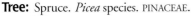

Tree: Spruce. *Picea* species. PINACEAE.
Description: About 45 species of medium- to slow-growing, upright, pyramid-shaped, coniferous evergreen trees, 75–150 ft. (23–46 m) tall, depending on species, often with whorled branches and radiating, shiny, deep blue green, stiff, round needles, to 3⁄4 in. (19 mm) long, and with blue gray, resinous bark.
Blooms/Cones: Male cones resemble feathery catkins, 1–3 in. (25–75 mm) long; female cones are dangling, elongated, and pointed, 2–6 in. (50–150 mm) long, with woody scales and pairs of 1-winged seed.
Plant hardiness: Zones 1–8, depending on species. All hardy to zone 6.
Soil: Moist, well-drained. Fertility: Rich–average. 5.5–7.0 pH.
Planting: Full–filtered sun. Space as recommended for species.
Care: Easy–moderate. Allow surface soil to dry between waterings until established. Avoid fertilizing. Prune only to shape in spring, removing half of new growth "candles." Propagate by cuttings, seed.
Features: Good choice for accents in containers, open landscapes. Maturing trees shade underfoliage, causing needle loss. Aphid, spider mite, gypsy, tussock moth and canker susceptible.

Tree: Stewartia. *Stewartia* species. THEACEAE.
Description: A few species of slow-growing, spreading, pyramid-shaped becoming round-crowned, open, deciduous shrubby trees, 10–25 ft. (3–7.6 m) tall, with shiny, deep green, oval, pointed, toothed leaves, 2–4 in. (50–100 mm) long, turning orange, red, yellow in autumn, and with flaking, red brown turning white bark. Species include Japanese stewartia, *S. pseudocamellia,* and tall stewartia, *S. monadelpha.*
Blooms/Fruit: Single, camellia-like white, wavy-edged, orange-centered flowers, 2–3 in. (50–75 mm) wide, in summer, form woody, brown, oval capsules containing wingless seed, in autumn.
Plant hardiness: Zones 6–9, depending on species.
Soil: Moist, well-drained humus. Fertility: Rich. 5.5–6.5 pH.
Planting: Full–filtered sun. Space 6–10 ft. (1.8–3 m) apart.
Care: Easy. Keep evenly moist. Fertilize annually in spring. Prune to shape in autumn. Avoid transplanting. Propagate by cuttings, layering, seed.
Features: Good choice for accents, beds, borders, foregrounds, mixed plantings in cottage, shade, woodland gardens. Pest, disease resistant.

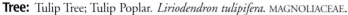

Tree: Sweet-Gum. *Liquidambar styraciflua.* HAMAMELIDACEAE.
Description: Slow-growing, broad, symmetrical, open, deciduous tree, to 120 ft. (35 m) tall and 50 ft. (15 m) wide, with glossy, maplelike, deep green, deeply toothed, leaves, 4–7 in. (10–18 cm) wide, turning red, purple, yellow in autumn, and with furrowed bark.
Blooms/Seed: Inconspicuous small flowers, in dangling clusters, in spring, form round, spiny, dangling seed clusters, in autumn.
Plant hardiness: Zones 5–9. Ground hardy zones 6–9.
Soil: Moist, well-drained. Fertility: Rich. 6.5–7.0 pH.
Planting: Full sun–partial shade. Space 25–30 ft. (7.5–9 m) apart. Transplant in spring.
Care: Easy. Allow surface soil to dry between waterings until established. Fertilize semi-annually spring–autumn. Prune sparingly in autumn. Transplants readily. Propagate by seed.
Features: Good choice for accent, specimen in most gardens. Shallow rooted. Chlorosis susceptible.

Tree: Tulip Tree; Tulip Poplar. *Liriodendron tulipifera.* MAGNOLIACEAE.
Description: Several cultivars of fast- to medium-growing, open, deciduous trees, to 120 ft. (37 m) tall, with maplelike, dark green, 5- or 7-lobed, toothed leaves, to 7 in. (18 cm) long, turning yellow gold tinged with rose in autumn.
Blooms/Seed: Fragrant, cup-shaped, apricot yellow–tinged green flowers, to 2 in. (50 mm) wide, in late spring on mature trees, form leathery seed clusters, to 3 in. (75 mm) long, in autumn.
Plant hardiness: Zones 4–9.
Soil: Moist, well-drained. Fertility: Rich. Add acidic compost. 6.0–6.5 pH.
Planting: Full sun. Space 15–25 ft. (4.5–7.5 m) apart.
Care: Easy. Allow surface soil to dry between waterings until established. Fertilize annually in spring until established. Prune in autumn. Propagate by cuttings, layering, seed.
Features: Good choice for accents, paths, screens in cottage, woodland gardens, lawns. Drops flowers, leaves, dry pods, requiring maintenance. Shallow rooted. Smog tolerant. Chlorosis susceptible.

Tree: Tupelo; Black Gum; Pepperidge; Sour Gum. *Nyssa sylvatica.* NYSSACEAE.
Description: Medium- to slow-growing, upright, pyramid-shaped then irregular, open, deciduous tree, to 100 ft. (30 m) tall, with shiny, deep green, oval leaves, to 5 in. (13 cm) long, turning purple, red in autumn, and with contorted branches and reddish bark. Related to cotton gum, *N. aquatica*, a wetland species.
Blooms/Fruit: Inconspicuous male and female flowers in spring form many deep blue, round, blueberry-like fruit, to ½ in. (12 mm) wide, in summer.
Plant hardiness: Zones 4–9.
Soil: Moist, well-drained. Fertility: Rich. 5.5–6.5 pH.
Planting: Full sun. Space 20–25 ft. (6–7.5 m) apart.
Care: Easy. Keep evenly moist. Fertilize annually in spring until established. Prune to direct growth in autumn. Protect from wind. Avoid transplanting. Propagate by layering, seed.
Features: Good choice for accents, backgrounds, paths in natural, woodland gardens. Good for seasonal color, shade. Fruit attracts birds. Drops staining fruit, requiring maintenance. Smog susceptible.

Tree: Willow. *Salix* species. SALICACEAE.

Description: About 300 species of fast-growing, usually upright and spreading, open, branching, brittle, deciduous trees, 6–100 ft. (1.8–30 m) tall, depending on species, with smooth, light green to yellow green, usually lance-shaped, pointed leaves, ¾–6 in. (19–150 mm) long, depending on species, turning yellow in autumn, and with red or pink turning gray, smooth becoming fissured bark.

Catkins/Fruit: Small catkins, ½–3 in. (12–75 mm) long, in spring, before leaves emerge or with leaf buds, form brown, woody capsules, ½–1 in. (12–25 mm) long, bearing hairy, tuftlike seed, in early summer.

Plant hardiness: Zones 1–10, depending on species.

Soil: Moist, well-drained. Fertility: Rich–low. 6.0–7.5 pH.

Planting: Full sun. Space as recommended for species.

Care: Easy–moderate. Keep evenly moist. Avoid fertilizing. Prune in autumn to shape, limit spread. Propagate by cuttings, seed.

Features: Good choice for accents, screens in landscapes and water gardens. Good for erosion control, temporary plantings. Shallow rooted. Very invasive. Susceptible to more than 120 insect pests and numerous diseases.

Tree: Yellowwood. *Cladrastis kentukea (C. lutea)*. FABACEAE (LEGUMINOSAE).

Description: A few cultivars of slow-growing, upright, round-crowned, open, deciduous trees, to 50 ft. (15 m) tall, with frondlike, yellow turning green leaves, to 1 ft. (30 cm) long, divided into dangling, 1- to 7-offset, walnutlike, oval leaflets, to 4 in. (10 cm) long, turning yellow in autumn, and with charcoal gray, smooth becoming furrowed bark.

Blooms/Fruit: Many showy, fragrant, white, pink, wisteria-like flowers, to 1 in. (25 mm) long, borne in dangling clusters, to 16 in. (40 cm) long, in early summer on mature trees, form brown, beanlike pods, 4 in. (10 cm) long, containing smooth seed, in autumn.

Plant hardiness: Zones 4–8. Best with winter chill, summer heat.

Soil: Moist, well-drained. Fertility: Average–low. 6.5–7.5 pH.

Planting: Full–filtered sun. Space 15–20 ft. (4.5–6 m) apart.

Care: Moderate. Allow surface soil to dry between waterings until established. Prune in summer. Propagate by cuttings, seed.

Features: Good choice for accents, containers in small-space gardens. Pest, disease resistant.

Tree: Zelkova, Japanese; Saw-Leaf Zelkova. *Zelkova serrata*. ULMACEAE.

Description: Several cultivars of medium-growing, elmlike, upright, vase-shaped, deciduous trees, to 100 ft. (30 m) tall, with deep green, textured, oval, pointed, veined, toothed leaves, to 5 in. (13 cm) long, turning brown, red, yellow in autumn, and with smooth becoming rough and exfoliating, gray bark.

Blooms/Fruit: Inconspicuous, clustered flowers, in early spring, form sparse mealy fruit, to ¼ in. (6 mm) wide, in late spring.

Plant hardiness: Zones 5–9. Best with winter chill.

Soil: Damp, well-drained. Fertility: Average–low. 6.0–7.5 pH.

Planting: Full sun. Space 20–25 ft. (6–7.5 m) apart.

Care: Easy. Allow surface soil to dry between waterings. Fertilize annually in spring. Prune to thin, train in autumn. Propagate by grafting, layering, seed.

Features: Good choice for allées, containers in bonsai, roadside plantings. Somewhat Dutch elm disease resistant. Aphid and scale susceptible.

USDA Plant Hardiness Around the World
North America

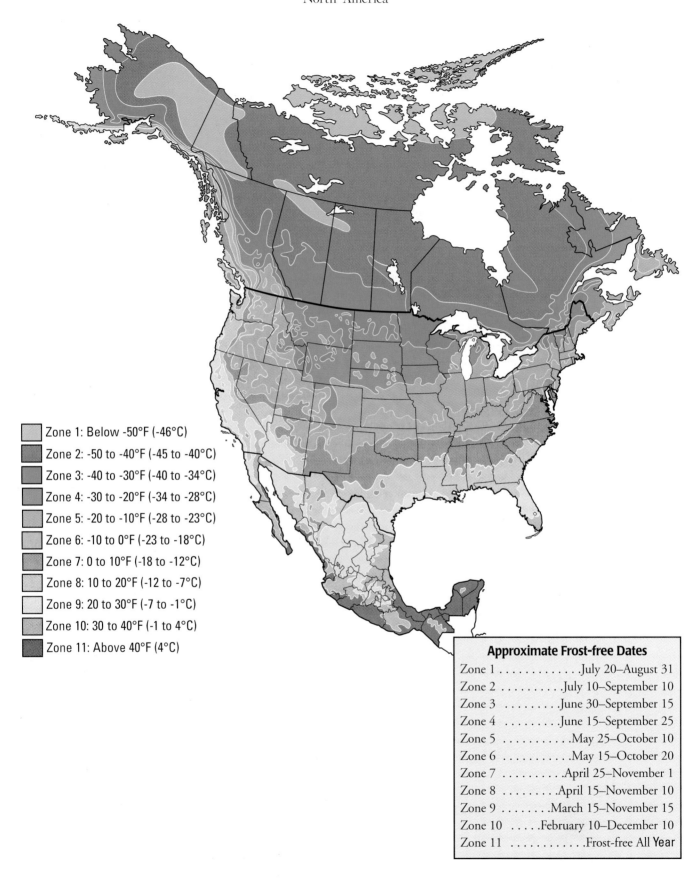

Zone 1: Below -50°F (-46°C)

Zone 2: -50 to -40°F (-45 to -40°C)

Zone 3: -40 to -30°F (-40 to -34°C)

Zone 4: -30 to -20°F (-34 to -28°C)

Zone 5: -20 to -10°F (-28 to -23°C)

Zone 6: -10 to 0°F (-23 to -18°C)

Zone 7: 0 to 10°F (-18 to -12°C)

Zone 8: 10 to 20°F (-12 to -7°C)

Zone 9: 20 to 30°F (-7 to -1°C)

Zone 10: 30 to 40°F (-1 to 4°C)

Zone 11: Above 40°F (4°C)

Approximate Frost-free Dates

Zone 1	July 20–August 31
Zone 2	July 10–September 10
Zone 3	June 30–September 15
Zone 4	June 15–September 25
Zone 5	May 25–October 10
Zone 6	May 15–October 20
Zone 7	April 25–November 1
Zone 8	April 15–November 10
Zone 9	March 15–November 15
Zone 10	February 10–December 10
Zone 11	Frost-free All Year

USDA Plant Hardiness Around the World
Australia

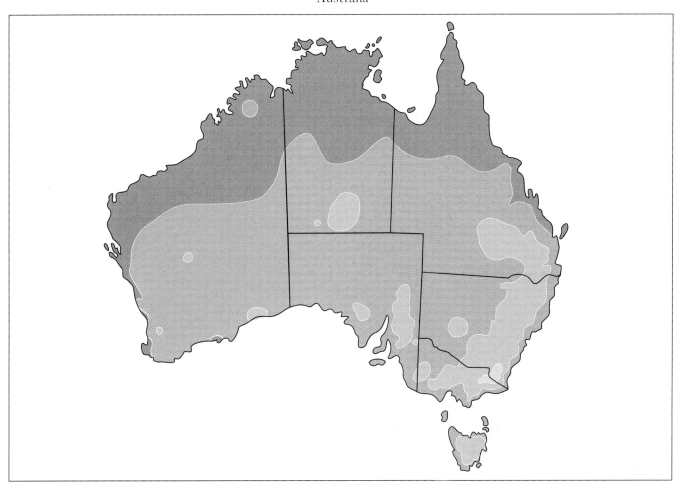

South Africa

New Zealand

Europe

ON-LINE   INDEX

INDEX

I N D E X